THE SEVERN TSUNAMI?

THE SEVERN TSUNAMI?

THE STORY OF BRITAIN'S GREATEST NATURAL DISASTER

MIKE HALL

In memory of the medieval carved Head of a Maiden, *hacked from its stand and stolen from St Thomas's Church, Redwick, at about 10 a.m. on Saturday, 9 June 2012. A witness to the flood disaster of 1607, what tales could she have told?*

First published 2013

The History Press
The Mill, Brimscombe Port
Stroud, Gloucestershire, GL5 2QG
www.thehistorypress.co.uk

British Library Cataloguing in Publication Data.
A catalogue record for this book is available from the British Library.

ISBN 978 0 7524 7015 3

Typesetting and origination by The History Press
Printed in Great Britain

CONTENTS

INTRODUCTION

'About nine of the clock in the morning, the same being most fairly and brightly spread, many of the inhabitants prepared themselves to their affairs.'

Then they might see afar off huge and mighty hills of water tumbling over one another as if the greatest mountains in the world had overwhelmed the low villages and marshy grounds. Sometimes it dazzled many of the spectators that they imagined it had been some fog or mist coming with a great swiftness towards them, and with such a smoke as if mountains were all on fire, and to the view of some it seemed as if millions of thousands of arrows had been shot forth all at one time. So violent and swift were the outrageous waves that in less than five hours' space most part of those countries (especially the places that lay low) were all overflown, and many hundreds of people, men, women and children, were quite devoured; nay, more, the farmers and husbandmen and shepherds might behold their goodly flocks swimming upon the waters – dead.

(*God's Warning to his people of England*, printed in 1607
by William Jones of Usk, Monmouthshire.)

One evening in April 2005 my wife Linda and I, staying at her parents' home in Almondsbury, north of Bristol, settled down to watch *Killer Wave of 1607*, a documentary in the BBC2 *Timewatch* series, giving an account of the flood that had devastated the lowland areas on either side of the Bristol

Redwick Church.

Channel in the early seventeenth century. We knew that this had affected nearby parts of South Gloucestershire and we were looking forward to seeing pictures of places that we knew well.

To be honest, we were a little disappointed. Much of the programme had been filmed in those strange foreign parts on the Welsh side of the Severn Bridge. A place called Redwick, which we had never heard of, figured prominently in some of the most dramatic reconstructions, but there was virtually nothing about Almondsbury, Olveston or South Gloucestershire in general. Little did we know that in less than two years' time we would be living in Redwick and attending the last of a series of events being held in the village to mark the 400th anniversary of the Great Flood.

Killer Wave of 1607 introduced to the wider public the theory proposed by Professor Simon Haslett and Dr Ted Bryant that the flood was caused by a tsunami. The programme had been filmed during the summer of 2004 and by the time it was broadcast its central thesis had been made poignantly topical by the awful events of Boxing Day in South East Asia and everyone watching knew what a tsunami was.

Some academics dispute Haslett and Bryant's conclusions, preferring to believe that the flood was the result of a storm surge. I am not a specialist in this field but I will try to summarise the evidence for both explanations in this book – which would not have been written if it had not been for the interest generated in the subject by the tsunami theory. I am grateful to all those (too numerous to list here) who have given me practical help and advice. Any errors of fact or interpretation are, of course, entirely my own work.

Mike Hall, Redwick, Monmouthshire, 2013.

Illustrations: All photographs are by Mike or Linda Hall unless otherwise stated. I am particularly grateful to Richard Jones for allowing me access to the pictures used in the *Flood 400* exhibition in 2007 (and for his advice and comments), also to Jane Gunn of Wedmore for her pictures of flooding on the Somerset Levels. The postcards used are from my own collection. Images sourced from Wikipedia are reproduced under the Creative Commons Attribution Share Alike licence. Finally, I could not have managed without the help of Linda and my younger daughter Elizabeth (who understand the minds of computers) in sorting the images for publication.

1

DATING AND MEASURING

Exactly when the flood happened has been a source of confusion over the years. It is usually referred to as the 1607 flood but many of the flood marks and other contemporary sources have it dated at 1606. The date of the event is given as 20 or 30 January, which makes marking the anniversary on the correct day problematic.

In Roman times the start of the year was reckoned to be the Ides (22) of March, a date infamous for the assassination of Julius Caesar. The Roman Catholic Church followed this practice until the sixteenth century and the fact that even now the tax year begins in April rather than January is a reminder of how things used to be. It took a while for the new system to become accepted, especially in Protestant countries. In England and Wales the New Year officially began on Lady Day (25 March). At the time of the flood, local people would have considered that they were nearing the end of 1606, while more 'up-to-date' folk in London and on the continent would have said it was 1607.

The other factor is the change from the Julian calendar to the Gregorian one. The old calendar had allowed for the fact that a year is actually 365¼ days long by introducing the concept of a Leap Year every four years, with an extra day on 29 February. However this adjustment was not precise enough and over the previous 1,500 years the calendar had got progressively out of phase with the seasons so that festivals such as Easter and Christmas had somehow drifted from their rightful place. Pope Gregory proposed to deal with this anomaly by declaring that in future, three out of the next four 'century years' would not be a leap year. 1600 was a leap year but 1700, 1800 and 1900 would not be. To get the calendar back in line with the seasons he decreed that ten days would be taken out altogether so that 4 October would be immediately followed by 15 October.

This new Gregorian calendar was introduced in Italy immediately, but once again other countries were slow to bring in the change. It was not done in England until 1752 when it famously led to riots and the slogan 'Give us back our ten days!' In this instance the Scots were ahead, introducing the new calendar in 1600, but even when their king, James VI, moved south in 1603 to become King James I of England (and Wales), the change was not made.

To sum up: the Great Flood occurred on 20 January 1606 (old style) and 30 January 1607 (new style).

The confusion has not gone away. In 2007, the *Flood 400* organisers put on a 'Wave of Bells' to commemorate the anniversary. Bells were rung in all the churches along the Welsh coast, from Rumney in the west to Chepstow in the east. This event took place on 20 January and I remember being told at great length by a steward in one of the reconstructed houses at the open-air museum at St Fagans that they should have done it on 30 January. However, there was also a Service of Commemoration, using words from the Prayer Book of the time, on 30 January, so the organisers of *Flood 400* wisely had both dates covered.

In his *West Country Weather Book*, which was published in 1995, author Barry Horton mirrored the uncertainty. He had looked at accounts of the flood in John Latimer's *Annals of Bristol* (1900–8), William Adams' *Chronicle of Bristol* (1910), G.E. Baker's article in *Bedfordshire Notes & Queries* (1884) and T.H. Baker's *Records of Seasons, Places and Phenomena* (1911) which gave a variety of permutations of date. 'As it was such a major event and many of the details are so similar,' he wrote in bewilderment, 'I can only conclude that these four writers have their years mixed up and it is the same event. Ironically, two of the writers who disagree on the year, do actually agree on the date of 20 January'. It would seem that Mr Horton did not know about Pope Gregory!

Finally, there is the similarly vexed question of measurement of distance. In 1607 (or 6) the metric system had not yet been invented. Inches, feet, yards and miles were the units used in the contemporary accounts and by people at the time. For me, to use metric would be perverse in the extreme.

I was not, despite what my former pupils might have believed, around at the time of the flood, but I am old enough to think more naturally in feet and inches. However, modern scientific research papers use the metric system and many readers will be more comfortable with it. I have compromised by using the same units as my sources while giving the alternative in brackets, which I hope will satisfy everybody!

2

RHINES
OR REENS?

The flat low-lying fields of the Somerset Levels and of the similar landscape on the Welsh side of the Severn Estuary are criss-crossed by a network of drainage ditches. In Wales these are called 'reens'. In Gloucestershire and Somerset the name for them sounds the same but is confusingly spelled 'rhines' or even 'rhynes'. This is a trap for the unwary, not least the Lancashire-based folk band who recorded an LP of songs to mark the 300th anniversary of the Battle of Sedgemoor in 1685. It was only after the record went on sale that someone pointed out to them that the word should not have been pronounced the same as the river! They probably used a rather different short word in response. I have used reen when referring to these channels on the Gwent Levels and rhines when referring to those on the English side.

A rhine near Olveston, Gloucestershire.

3

CONTEMPORARY SOURCES

Researchers are fortunate that the flood happened when the country was more literate than at any period since the Romans. It was the time of Shakespeare's plays and the King James Bible. There were no newspapers but increasingly pamphlets reporting and commenting on current events were being produced in London. St Paul's churchyard had become a focus for the printing of these and many of them had an apocalyptic religious flavour. Typical of these was *God's Warning to His People* which began with 'many are the doom warnings of destruction which the Almighty God hath lately scourged this our Kingdom with; and many more are the threatening tokens of his heavy wrath extended towards us'. Moral lessons were pointed out, such as 'many men that were rich in the morning when they rose out of their beds were made poor before noon the same day'. For the writers of these pamphlets, the disaster was seen as a judgement by God on his sinful people.

These publications hardly had snappy concise titles. The full title of *God's Warning to His People* continued *Wherein is related most Wonderfull and Miraculous works, by the late overflowing of the Waters, in the Countryes of Somerset and Gloucester, the Counties of Munmoth, Glamorgan, Carmarthen and Cardigan with divers other places in South Wales* – which says it all, really! *Newes out of Summerset-shire* was 'a *true report of certaine wonderfull ouerflowing of Waters now lately in Summerset-shire, Norfolke and other places of England: destroying many thousands of men, women and children, overthrowing and bearing downe upon whole townes and villages, and drowning infinite numbers of sheepe*

Artist's impression of the woodcut that appeared on a contemporary pamphlet titled *Lamentable Newes out of Monmouthshire in Wales.*

and other Cattle'. Lamentable Newes out of Monmouthshire had a similarly long-winded full title. They shared the same woodcut illustration, a scene reputedly showing the tower of Nash Church surrounded by floodwaters that has become the defining visual image of the event.

Other important written sources include a vivid description of events in North Devon written by Adam Wyatt, the town clerk of Barnstaple, and details from the town's parish registers. The registers of Arlingham in Gloucestershire give a dramatic account of both the saving and loss of life, while the Vicar of Almondsbury's report includes significant meteorological information. The diary of Walter Yonge of Colyton and Axminster, though hardly an eyewitness, also gives some detail absent from other sources, as does Camden's *Britannia* and some poems by John Stradling in his book *Epigrams*.

All these sources have been pored over by competing academics, searching for that vital clue to help determine the cause of the event. For example, the description in *God's Warning ...*, quoted at the beginning of this book, is seen by many as evoking visions of an advancing tsunami off the coast of Thailand in the bright sunshine of 26 December 2004. There are full details and extracts from these documents at www.website.lineout.net which seems to be the most comprehensive source on the internet for information on the flood. Where I have quoted from these publications, I have modernised the spelling and punctuation for ease of reading but this site has links to the original text for those who need it.

Many churches in the affected area have near-contemporary memorials. There are flood marks at Peterstone, Nash and Redwick in Monmouthshire, a brass plaque with rustic lettering at Goldcliff, a stone one at St Brides Wentloog and a board at Kingston Seymour in Somerset. A second memorial there gives details of a subsequent flood which led the inhabitants of nearby Yatton to take out a lawsuit to try to recoup their losses of crops and livestock after the sea wall gave way and saltwater covered their fields. Many of the places flooded in 1607 had suffered the same fate before and would do again, not least in the Somerset Levels, much of which was under water at the time of writing.

4

1607 –
AN 'INTERESTING' YEAR

It is said by some (though disputed by others) that the Chinese have a curse which reads 'may you live in interesting times'. For many, 1607 was an 'interesting' year. It began with a financial crisis on 13 January: the Bank of Genoa crashed after the announcement of national bankruptcy in Spain.

The same month, ships waiting to sail from England to America were prevented from sailing by stormy weather at sea. Later in the year, colonists were to make landfall on the coast of Virginia, move up the James River and establish Jamestown, the first permanent English settlement in the New World.

Jamestown was, of course, named after King James I, who had been King of England since 1603, having previously been James VI of Scotland. In 1605 he had survived the attempt on his life in the Gunpowder Plot of Guy Fawkes and his fellow conspirators. In 1606, Shakespeare's *Macbeth* was published, a work so ill-omened that even today members of the acting profession dare not speak its name.

And then there was the Great Flood …

Appledore in North Devon was probably the first place to suffer the fury of the giant waves that terrible morning. If there was anyone in the steep, sloping churchyard at Instow on the opposite side of the river, they probably would not at first have paid much attention to the white water over the bar at its mouth – that would have been a familiar sight. But this wave just kept on coming, growing higher and more destructive as it came towards the shore. Later, the pamphlet *More Strange News* would describe how 'many houses were overthrown and sunk', as the wall of water broke over, demolishing them and 'a ship of some three score tons, being ready to hoist sail and being well-laden, was driven by this tempest beyond all water-mark and is never likely to be brought back again'. The wave struck perpendicular to the shore and then peeled along it before inflicting considerable damage at Instow, where a new jetty had to be built after the disaster.

Using the evidence of date stones, Haslett and Bryant (2004) suggest that the oldest surviving building on the seafront in Appledore is Port Cottage, built around 1750. Around Irsha Street and the Royal George pub, the area that took the full force of the wave as it struck, there are no older buildings. At Instow, it is probably Sailors' Rest Cottage (dated 1640, thirty-three years after the flood). They conclude that 'the events of 1607 may have lasted a considerable time in the folk memory … and reconstruction might have been understandably slow to follow'.

The onrushing waters followed the Taw Valley inland to Barnstaple. Robert Langdon, the parish clerk, described how 'there was such a mighty storm and tempest from the river with the coming of the tide that it caused much loss of goods and houses, to the value of a thousand pounds … The storm began at three o'clock in the morning and continued till twelve.'

View from Instow churchyard.

A document in the North Devon Record Office (ref: NDRO.B12/1), quoted by Haslett and Bryant, states that there was:

A very great flood. Water came up in Southgate Street and in Wilstreet. It came to Appley's fore door and run out through the house into the garden there and made great spoil. The water flowed more than half way up Maiden Street and then went into their houses. Also it came up at the lower end of Cross Street so far as Mr Takles hall door. The tombstone upon the Quay was covered clean over with water – by report it was higher by five or six feet than ever remembered by those now living.

West of the Quay, a house belonging to a Mr Collybear was badly damaged, as was Mr Stanberie's to the east. Nearby some of the first deaths took place:

[the wave] threw down the whole house wherein James Frost did dwell, whereby himself was slain with the fall of the roof and two children slain with the falling of the walls. All the walls between that and the Castle fell and the top of the house of the horse mill began to cleave asunder and likely to have fallen down if the Spil[way]l of the Mill, which was very strong, had not supported.

What happened in Barnstaple is well documented. Besides these accounts of the disaster, there are two others – by the town clerk, Adam Wyatt (Somerset Record Office, SF 4051) and one Tristram Risdon, writing in 1620. These will be referred to later.

Meanwhile, the monster waves were also wreaking havoc on the Welsh side of the Severn Estuary. In a matter of minutes, the beach near Ogmore Castle in the Vale of Glamorgan was engulfed in rocks and boulders in such a way that researchers in the twenty-first century concluded that a tsunami must have been responsible. Elsewhere, cliffs were rapidly eroded by the force of the water. One of these places was Sully, west of Cardiff, where the narrowing of the Bristol Channel would have constricted the wave and forced it to increase in height, becoming even more dangerous. At Aberthaw, now the site of a power station that is a prominent landmark seen from shipping in the estuary, the recently built seawall was, according to the poet John Stradling, 'overcome and wholly torn apart'. The previous year, Stradling had written a poem about this as 'constructed for the containment of the Severn, a herculean labour completed within five months'.

At Cardiff, St Mary's Church, which stood beside the River Taff, was another victim. A contemporary chronicler wrote that 'a greater part of the church … was beaten down with the water'. As Dennis Morgan wrote in *Discovering Cardiff's Past*, 'from this document arose a myth that the flood spelt the end for the mother church'. Speed's map of 1610 shows the church more or less intact but he notes that the river was 'a foe of St Mary's … undermining her foundations and threatening her fall'. It would appear that the flood in 1607 removed a corner of the churchyard and the townspeople subsequently preferred to spend money on St John's, which was in a more secure location towards the castle. St Mary's was used less and less and was further damaged during the Civil War. By 1678, the central tower had collapsed through the roof and the building was a mere shell. Burials continued in what remained of the churchyard until 1707 and, Morgan adds, 'children were baptised in the ruins as late as the 1730s'. An outline in lighter stone on the side of the Prince of Wales pub in Wood Street (near the Bus Station) is believed to mark the approximate position of where the church once stood.

The flood plain between the town and the Bristol Channel was inundated. The water overtopped the ancient sea banks and came as far inland as Adamsdown and Splott, areas which later became densely

Outline of former St Mary's Church, Cardiff.

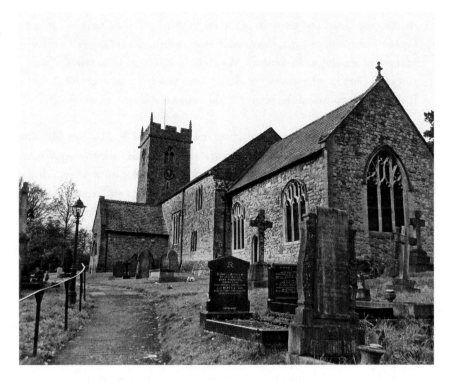

Rumney Church, near Cardiff.

populated working-class suburbs but which in 1607 were almost uninhabited. The flood reached as far inland as Llandaff, four miles away, where a contemporary chronicler noted that 'Mistress Matthews lost 400 sheep [and] no-one was spared from the impact of the deluge'.

East of Cardiff, the fields of Rumney parish (now just another suburb) were also engulfed, despite fairly recent repairs to the sea wall. The historian J.R.L. Allen quotes from the records of the Court of Augmentations for 25 February 1590/1 (depending on how New Year was defined) which said: 'There is a wall between the sea and the lordship [manor] for the defence of the same, which wall being about two years past in great decay was by commission new made and placed more into land than it was.' Bodies were washed up here and subsequently buried in a communal grave near the church.

In 1610, Harry Dunne of Rumney was in court attempting to prove his title to the land he farmed. Unfortunately for Dunne, according to the court records:

At the great flood and invasion of the sea in those parts, the house of John Dunne [the former owner, presumably Harry's father] was broken by force of the said sea and, at that instant, the cupboards, chests and coffers of the said John Dunne, wherein the evidences, writings and copies of the Court Rolls which concerned the premises, were carried away in the said flood.

Eastwards again and the water reached the bottom of St Mellons Hill and had swamped the villages of Peterstone and St Brides Wentloog. We are now on the edge of the Gwent Levels, that extensive area of reclaimed land on either side of the estuary of the River Usk that suffered as badly as anywhere on the Welsh side of the Bristol Channel. Its churches to this day bear the flood marks and memorials to a force of nature, to which this area was particularly vulnerable.

Archdeacon Coxe, an antiquarian whose account of his travels through Monmouthshire nearly 200 years after the flood is a rich source of topographical and historical detail, captured the special character of this unique area. He wrote:

The ground is cut into parallel ditches, in some of which the water stagnates, in others it runs in perpetual streams called reens, which fall into the sea through flood-gates or gouts. The roads leading through these flat marshes are straight, narrow and pitched, which exhausts the patience of the traveller.

In a paragraph that may reflect the legacy of 1607 he adds, 'these marshes, being only inhabited by farmers and labourers, contain very few houses and cottages ... In former times the population must have been considerable, because the churches are large and capable of containing great congregations, though now reduced to forty or fifty persons'.

Lamentable Newes out of Monmouthshire and other pamphlets contain a number of incidents that are said to have happened in Monmouthshire during the Great Flood. Most of these would have happened here on the Levels but cannot now be precisely located. One example is the story of 'Mistress Van, a wealthy woman who lived four miles from the sea who, although she saw the wave approaching from her house, could not get upstairs before it rushed through and drowned her'. Some later writers place her at Llandaff but another source suggests the location as being near Marshfield, Newport. The Lewis family of Van near Caerphilly were well known in South Wales in the sixteenth and seventeenth centuries.

The website of the National Library of Wales (www.llgc.org.uk) describes the family's distinguishing features as 'a lengthy pedigree and a marvellous aptitude for the acquisition of property'.

Pamphlet readers were told of 'a maid child, not passing the age of four, whose mother, perceiving the waters to break so fast into her house, and not being able to escape it, and having no clothes on, set it upon a beam of the house, to save it from being drowned'. This tale reads like a biblical miracle, for it goes on: 'And the waters rushing in a pace, a little chicken as it seemeth, flew unto the child and was found in her bosom when help came to take her down and, by the heat thereof, as it is thought, preserved the child's life'. Another heart-warming tale from the county concerns …

> a little child affirmed to have been cast upon land in a cradle with a cat, the which was discerned (as it came floating to the shore) to leap from one side of the cradle unto the other, even as if she had been appointed steersman to preserve the small barque from the waves' fury.

Yet another miracle escape was achieved by the Monmouthshire man and woman who …

> having taken to a tree for their succour, espying nothing but death before their eyes, at last (among other things which were carried along) perceived a tub of great bigness to come nearer and nearer unto them, until it rested upon the tree wherein they were, committed themselves, and were carried safe until they were cast upon the dry shore.

The hero of the hour in Monmouthshire must have been the main landowner locally, Lord Herbert of Pencoed Castle near Llanmartin, who, the chronicles record, 'sent out boats to relieve the distress … himself going to such houses as he could to minister to the provision of meat and other necessities.' Without this noble and altruistic action, many more would have perished from starvation or cold in the days that followed.

The defences of the Gwent Levels were in the hands of the Commissioners of Sewers, originally established in the time of King Henry IV and invested with powers, as historian Charles Heath put it in 1829, 'equal, if not superior to the Sovereign', which shows the importance the Crown gave to protecting this rich farmland. Their duty was to 'secure the prompt obedience of tenants and landholders in repairing the first breaches or injuries of dykes and sea walls' – but what happened in 1607 was clearly well beyond what could have been predicted.

It was the same story on the other side of the Bristol Channel in Somerset. As the wave rushed in, the sea wall at Burnham collapsed and the water rolled over the low-lying levels and moors inland. The coastal village of Brean was swallowed up, with seven of its nine houses demolished and twenty-six inhabitants drowned. Twenty-eight died at Huntspill and the church at Kingston Seymour was flooded to the depth of five feet and remained so for the next ten days. The floods reached Bridgwater and across the flat Somerset Levels all the way to Glastonbury Tor, inundating villages and farmland as they went. In Glastonbury it reached St Benedict's Church. Things were made worse by the fact that, beyond the dunes and defences along the coast, the land actually slopes downward as you go inland. What defences there were had been the responsibility of the great churches of Wells and Glastonbury and may have fallen into disrepair after the Dissolution of the Monasteries under Henry VIII.

Flooding on the Somerset Levels. (idleformat, Flickr)

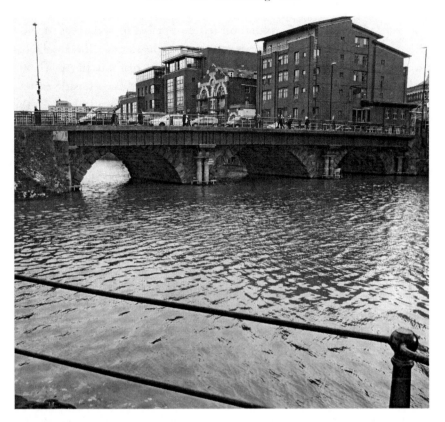

Bristol Bridge.

The proud city of Bristol, despite being set back from the Severn Estuary, was not safe from the rising waters. Here the problem was made worse by the partial damming of the incoming tide by Bristol Bridge. Instead, the tide overflowed into Redcliffe Street, Temple Street and Thomas Street, flooding them to the depth of several feet in places. It was said that a boat of five tons was carried from the river towards St Nicholas Church and was only prevented from entering the crypt by the skill of an oarsman on board. St Stephen's Church and the quay were also flooded, leading to the loss of valuable goods stored in cellars and warehouses. One contemporary account described how 'people of the town were enforced to be carried in boats, by and down the said city, about their business in the fair time there'.

Barry Horton in his *West Country Weather Book* notes that this was not the end of Bristol's problems. Not surprisingly, perhaps, the harvest in 1607 was very poor and the Corporation felt compelled to take steps to avert the danger of famine. Corn prices were very high after the flood and what livestock had survived the disaster also ran short of food. In April 1608 a thousand bushels of wheat were bought in, £1,000 set aside to buy corn from Holland and a further £300 for supplies from Ireland. In the summer of 1610 there was a drought and the price of wheat rose to 72s a quarter, causing what Latimer's *Annals* describes as 'fearful distress among the poor'.

North of Bristol, the low-lying land on both sides of the Severn was flooded, almost all the way up to Gloucester, and the area around Redwick (Gloucestershire) and Pilning was badly affected. The Vicar of Almondsbury later wrote a graphic account of what happened. The parish register at Arlingham recorded twenty deaths and at Chepstow, on the Welsh side of the river, there were two deaths reported.

As Chris Witts describes in *Disasters on the Severn* (2002):

Both sides of the Severn were covered by water for a distance of six miles inland. It is estimated that 500 people perished that day, besides thousands of animals. One eyewitness said it was a strange sight to see the carcasses of wild animals, foxes, rabbits, rats, etc., floating together with dead people and cattle.

In the aftermath of the disaster the lowland areas around the Bristol Channel presented a scene of utter devastation as *God's Warning to his people of England* summed up vividly:

Divers churches lie hidden in the waters. Of some of them the tops are to be seen, of others nothing at all but the very tops of the steeples and of some nothing at all, neither steeple nor nothing else. Also, many young scholars in many places stood in great perplexity. Some of them, venturing home to their parents, were drowned on the way. Others, staying behind in churches, did climb up to the tops of steeples, where they were very near starved to death for want of food and fire. Many, by the help of boards and planks of wood, swam to dry land and so were preserved from untimely death. Many had boats brought them, some ten miles, some fifteen, some twenty, where there was never seen any boats before.

Significantly perhaps – or by coincidence – flooding also occurred on the evening of the same day on the opposite side of the country. Water was

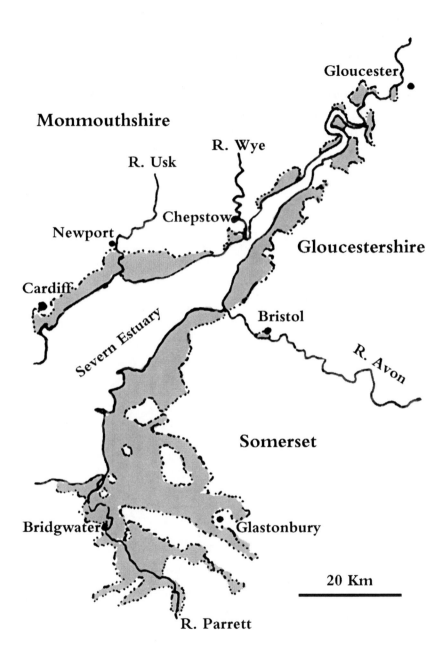

Simplified map of areas inundated in 1607. (Based on map in Rippon S., *The Severn Estuary*: Leicester University Press, 1997)

said to have broken out of an old breach and overflowed marshland near King's Lynn in Norfolk. Several people drowned and a vivid contemporary account describes 'houses up to their middles in water, joining with land waters that fell from the high grounds.' A tsunami would not have hit the fenland of Norfolk as well as the West Country and South Wales. Was the disaster simply the result of bad weather and a storm surge — or is there some other explanation?

5

THE CAUSE
OF THE DISASTER

In the aftermath of a disaster there are two questions that are always asked: What caused it to happen? What can be done to prevent it happening again? In the case of the Great Flood, the modern scientific debate centres around whether it was caused by a storm surge or a tsunami – but many in 1607 had no doubt: it was the result of 'the sinfulness of Man and his disobedience of God's Law'.

The author of *Woeful Newes From Wales* expressed this view in typical fashion:

What shall I say concerning the contempt of the Ministry of the Word and the manifold wrongs continually offered even unto the most reverend and faithful Ministers of the same? Is it the covetousness of our own hard-hearted age? Doth it not destroy and corrupt daily more and more, both Church and Common Weal among us? Hath it not stolen almost into every corner and crept well near into every heart, marring all where it cometh?

But he is blind who noteth not the several kinds of oppression everywhere practised and the lying and dissimulation everywhere used. In a word idleness, one of those sins which caused Sodom to be destroyed, is most palpably to be noted in all states and conditions of men among us, both in Church and Common Weal, while the Clergy doeth nothing but look for livings and leave the labours of their function; and the gentry esteem more of their hawks, hounds and other vainer pleasures than the godly discharging of their offices wherein the Lord has set them.

And shall we then imagine that they were only good that are gone in the calamity of waters? Certainly, as I make no question but God hath had His faithful servants among them, so I doubt not but the greater part of them were even as the rest of our Nation is at this day: lewd and profane wretches whom the Lord hath thus plagued for to recall us, if it be possible, from our filthy practices lest all at once he be provoked to pour down the full vials of his wrath upon us.

And therefore, if we be wise, let other men's harms make us wary, less custom in vice make it grow even another nature to us. Wherefore above all things, let us take heed that long escape of punishment or the vain hope of long life do not delude us and make us run on still into our sins. For our life is but like the gourd of Jonas or the pilgrimage of Jacob, the days thereof are as few as evil. Yea, it is like unto the vision of Esdras, goodly to look upon, but vanished in a moment.

Setting aside the theory that the victims of the Great Flood were 'lewd and profane wretches' who deserved what they got, now we move on to the tsunami versus the storm surge debate. The belief that the disaster was the result of extreme weather and a storm surge up the Bristol Channel has been around for a long time but it was the publication of research by Haslett and Bryant and the *Timewatch* television programme in 2005 that really stimulated public interest in the idea of a tsunami.

Haslett and Bryant set out their evidence in a series of scientific papers, most notably in the journal *Archaeology in the Severn Estuary* in 2002 and 2004. Much of the discussion is highly technical and can only be summarised here but there are fuller details available on the internet.

They suggest that proponents of the storm surge hypothesis are ignoring significant detail in the contemporary accounts: that the disaster occurred on a day that was 'most fairly and brightly spread' – fine weather that was unlikely to accompany a storm or strong winds. We are told that 'many of the inhabitants prepared themselves to their affairs'. In other words, it was business as usual. The ship that was wrecked at Appledore, for example, would not have been about to set sail into waters that were known to be dangerous at the best of times, if a storm was coming up from the west.

Another factor they cite is that the waves inundated the coastal lowlands 'with a swiftness so incredible that no greyhound could have escaped by running before them', and appeared as 'mighty hills of water tumbling over one another in such sort as if the greatest mountains in the world had overwhelmed the low villages or marshy grounds'. They also state that:

[it] dazzled many of the spectators that they imagined it had been some fog or mist coming with great swiftness towards them and with such smoke as if mountains were all on fire and to the view of some it seemed as if myriads of arrows had been shot forth all at one time.

This description refers to the sparks that were seen to come off the top of the wave and all these features are found in eyewitness accounts of tsunamis, not only the 2004 disaster but also that associated with the eruption of Krakatoa in 1883. In 1929 when a tsunami affected the Burin Peninsula in Newfoundland the wave crest was reported as shining like the headlights of a car, and in 1998 the wave of a tsunami in Papua New Guinea was described as 'frothing and sparkling'. In both 1607 and 2004, the sea receded unexpectedly before the tsunami struck and on both occasions unwary crowds who had gathered on beaches to see what was happening were drowned as the sea crashed onto the shore a few minutes later.

Most of the contemporary accounts mention strong winds. At first glance, this might appear to back up the storm surge theory, but in their 2004 article, Haslett and Bryant point out that computer modelling requires hurricane winds of 80 miles (125km) per hour to reconstruct the original flooding. 'Such winds alone would result in widespread damage and casualties,' they wrote, 'but there is no mention of either in any historical document that we have seen'.

Appledore (early twentieth century).

In typically cautious researchers' language they conclude that 'the ambiguity of the regional meteorological conditions, the lack of documentary evidence for hurricane winds and the nature of the damage inflicted do not allow us to reject the tsunami hypothesis for the origin of the 1607 flood.'

The same historical sources tell us that the waters reached the foot of Glastonbury Tor, some 14 miles inland, and flooded houses. This is possible because, as already mentioned, the surface of the Somerset Levels slopes away from the coast so, when the tsunami wave broke and collapsed, the floodwater reached further inland rather than going back towards the sea.

Haslett and Bryant also quote geological evidence, including huge boulders on beaches in South Wales that had clearly been displaced by massive forces, and a layer of sand, shells and stones intruded into otherwise constant and uniform mud deposits found in boreholes from Devon to Gloucestershire and on the Gower Peninsula. This, they suggest, was also caused by exceptionally high water velocities throughout the Severn Estuary, consistent with a tsunami rather than a storm surge. They refer to two large pieces of land to the north of Bristol by the Severn that had been washed away. Worryingly perhaps, one of these is where the foundations of the Second Severn Crossing are today and the other is the reservoir for Oldbury Nuclear Power Station. In addition, the extensive erosion of saltmarsh and truncation of spurs of land observed in the area also support the tsunami thesis.

Glastonbury Tor.

But where would such a tsunami have originated? Haslett and Bryant postulate that a landslide off the continental shelf between Ireland and Cornwall may have been the culprit. They also noted a geological fault system off the coast of southern Ireland. They pointed out that this had experienced an earthquake bigger than magnitude 4 on the Richter scale in 1980. This scale is, of course, a logarithmic one with each point on the scale ten times more severe than the previous one, and one of the same intensity in 1607 would not have had such dire consequences. However, it is possible that such a quake could have happened, triggering an underwater landslide that set off the tsunami.

Haslett and Bryant wrote in an article in *The Journal of Geology* that their fieldwork 'adds to the recent evidence juxtaposing the geological and historic records. The fact that the signatures of tsunami are found in the Bristol Channel up to the more sheltered Severn Estuary is surprising because the north-west European coast in general is not considered tsunami-prone.'

It would seem that the tsunami theory has a lot to commend it, but it has its critics. One of the most impassioned, perhaps, is the author of *Dicmortimer's Blog* (www.dicmortimer.wordpress.com), who takes a somewhat personal aim at one of Haslett and Bryant's supporters. Having made a few necessary corrections to the punctuation, I quote directly:

Shortly after the Indian Ocean tsunami, caused by the third largest earthquake ever recorded (magnitude 9.2), Michael Disney, Professor of Astronomy at Cardiff University, claimed loudly that there had been a similar event in the Severn Estuary 400 years previously, and dubbed the well-documented Great Flood of 1607 the Cardiff tsunami.

Disney (now retired) is one of many academics at Cardiff over the years whose chief aim seems to be to garner eye-catching headlines in the tabloid press in the mistaken belief that this will raise the university's profile. In fact, all he and his colleagues ever achieve is to damage its reputation as a serious institution, as Cardiff's slide down the Higher Education ranking tables attests. His intervention was a major mistake; not only because it was a brazen attempt to muscle in on the Indian Ocean catastrophe that had just killed 30,000 people; but also because it was plain wrong. There was no 'Cardiff Tsunami' in 1607 – it was far more frightening than that … The 1607 flood was not as exciting or as newsworthy as a tsunami – it was just geography. I think it is a disgrace to ride the bandwagon of topical tragedies as a way to shoe-horn yourself into higher Google rankings, I really do.

There is, possibly, some political agenda going on here that I do not understand, but it is a pity that 'Dicmortimer' comes across as so hysterical because he may have a point somewhere. As he rightly says:

> It would take an Atlantic earthquake of at least magnitude 7 to generate any sort of tsunami up the Severn. Such an earthquake would have been felt across the whole of north-west Europe and tsunamis would have hit the coasts of Ireland, Pembrokeshire, Cornwall, Brittany and all points south to Portugal. None of this happened. Not one contemporary source reported earth tremors or unusually large waves. No; this was a concurrence of quite common phenomena that is all too capable of happening again; an exceptionally high spring tide in the Severn, combined with a deep low-pressure Atlantic storm surge.

The same point is made with more restraint and greater authority in *1607 Bristol Channel Floods: 400 Year Retrospective Special Report* published by Risk Management Solutions (RMS) in 2007, which states that:

> While there are some descriptions of the arriving flood that have elements comparable to a tsunami, there are many other descriptions that discount the tsunami explanation. In the ten surviving accounts of the flood, there is only one that suggests a tsunami and this is also, perhaps not coincidentally, the account which contains the greatest religiosity in style and content ... *God's Warning to his People of England.*

The RMS report sees little evidence for the sort of off-shore earthquake needed to generate such a massive tsunami. It points out that the largest quake to have occurred in the vicinity of the British Isles was the 1931 North Sea quake, measuring 5.5 on the Richter scale. This was felt strongly in countries bordering the North Sea and caused minor damage down the east coast of England from Yorkshire to Norfolk. Significantly, it was still far too small to have generated a tsunami.

The report states that to generate a sufficiently large tsunami a quake of the magnitude of 7.5 or more would have been needed, which would have been 200 times more powerful than the largest known earthquake in north-west Europe. Even an earthquake at 6 on the Richter scale would have been felt all over the region. It concludes: 'There was no such earthquake at the time of the 1607 Bristol Channel Floods. There is also no record of a tsunami in 1607 along any of the other coasts from the Isles of Scilly to Cornwall to Brittany to Southern Ireland.' It goes on to point out that the 8.5 magnitude Lisbon earthquake caused catastrophic damage in southern Portugal and seiching (oscillation of lake waters) in Britain and Scandinavia but, although noticed at low tide in Cornwall, was not observed in the Bristol Channel. The report concludes that 'the evidence is consistent with the 1607 Bristol Channel Floods being a storm surge focused up the Severn Estuary'.

For RMS an extreme spring tide was a crucial factor. One was due that day, as is evidenced by the Vicar of Almondsbury, who noted that 'the river of Severn rose upon a sodeyn Tuesday morning, the 20th January, being the full prime day and the highest tide after the change of the moon'. An analysis of tidal records and astronomical calculations was carried out by K. Horsborough and M. Horritt and published in the specialist journal *Weather* in 2006. This concluded that the highest tide in the month at Avonmouth would have been at 9 a.m. on the 30th, estimated at 7.86 metres (around 20 feet) above Ordnance Datum (AOD). Twice a month, the high tides are at their highest (spring tides) and this tide was exceptionally high because 'the semi-diurnal tidal forces were at their most extreme'. This means that the sun and the moon were both overhead at the equator and the moon at its closest to the earth, a point known as its perigee. The 27 January 1607 marked the second closest perigee of the year, and a full moon. The highest tides follow two or three days later, so the morning of the 30th would have been the highest of the season. This conjunction happens approximately every four and a half years.

The whole thing was put more picturesquely by poet John Stradling who was caught by the flood at Aust and wrote to Thomas Luttrell at Dunster: 'If you crave to understand the Severn's unwonted floods, what causes they have and the source of this madness, the common people attribute it to the moon and the driving winds, they rise their mind no higher'.

The tide that morning was indeed extremely high but it should be noted that it was still only a few inches higher than many other tides in previous years. The Gwent and Somerset Levels are about fifteen feet above mean sea level. Such a high tide would be above this but not really enough to flow over the top of the sea walls causing such great devastation.

There was also the chance that it was very windy. Strong winds from the south-west can, under certain circumstances, drive water into the Irish Sea and raise sea levels. This is particularly significant in shallow extremities

View from Almondsbury Hill over the Severn Levels.

such as Morecambe Bay and the Severn Estuary. Surges of over three feet can be expected perhaps ten times a year. In January 1991 a surge peak of more than twice that was recorded at Heysham. Such surges would not be significant at ordinary tides and even at the highest tides the sea walls, if properly maintained, should be able to cope. Yet if such a surge had happened that morning, combined with the highest tide for years, the story just might have been different. Such a surge caused the destructive East Coast floods of 1953. It may also be relevant to point out that, although Haslett and Bryant were excited by unusual deposits on Severn Estuary beaches that they interpreted as being the result of a tsunami, layers extracted at Rumney Great Wharf and North Devon, referred to in the *Timewatch* documentary, yielded radiocarbon dates that were too recent to have been laid down by the 1607 flood and are considered more likely to have been the result of the Great Storm of 1703.

Burton's Admirable Curiosities states that:

> A mighty west wind continuing sixteen hours brought the sea into the Severn (after a great rain and a tide) with such violence that it began to overflow its banks from the Mount in Cornwall along both sides into Somerset and Gloucestershire. In some places the water rose three foot, in others five or seven, and in some towns and villages higher than the tops of the houses; so that eighty people were drowned, cattle, divers churches and parishes overwhelmed, with much harm in Wales, the damage being reckoned above £20,000.

Camden's *Britannia*, published later in 1607, also refers to the wind.

> For the Severn Sea after a Spring Tide being driven back by a south-west wind (which continued three days without intermission) and then again repulsed by a very forcible sea wind, it raged with such a tide, as to overflow all this lower tract, and also that of Somersetshire over against it; undermining several houses and overwhelming a considerable number of cattle and men.

In North Devon, the Barnstaple parish register recorded that a windstorm had begun 'at three o'clock in the morning and continued till twelve the same day'. Perhaps the crew of that ship which was wrecked at nearby Appledore were not as foresighted as at first it seemed!

It may even be possible to use the contemporary accounts to reconstruct the changing wind direction during the day. There is the tale from Glamorgan of a blind man washed out of his house still in his bed, catching hold of a rafter of a house 'swimming by the fierceness of the winds, then blowing easternly' and then being driven safely to land again. This indicates, the RMS report suggests 'that the centre of the storm had passed and that he was now on its northern side.' From the vicar of Almondsbury's account we learn that 'the morning tide was higher than the evening tide by nine foot [about 3m] of water.' This is greater than could be caused by a storm surge alone but might be the result of the water being affected by an easterly wind springing up later in the day.

Wind patterns that fateful January day may also explain the apparent anomaly of flooding in Norfolk that cannot possibly be related to a tsunami. The suggestion is that there was a strong north-easterly onshore wind at the same time as the extreme tide. The RMS report concludes that 'this must have been on the north side of the centre of an extra-tropical cyclone' and adds that 'the last time King's Lynn was flooded on its own was on 11 January 1978 when a slow-moving low pressure system was located to the south-east of a major anticyclone, creating a very strong pressure gradient and north-easterly winds on its northern side.'

All this appears to contradict the writer of *God's Warning* who, you will remember, described 'the sun being most fairly and brightly spread' at nine o'clock. Some weather experts suggest that this could be a description of what the RMS report calls 'one class of rapidly intensifying extra tropical cyclone that had gathered a dry sector intrusion as a result of very cold dry air from above the tropopause [the layer of the atmosphere about seven miles above the earth's surface] gaining entry into the heart of the storm'. It quotes as an example the windstorm, codenamed Lothar, which hit Paris on Boxing Day 1999. However, it should be repeated that none of the contemporary accounts speak of significant wind damage.

Although dramatic, the flooding appears to have taken longer to cover the area than a tsunami should have done. *God's Warning* states that it took five hours for 'most parts ... especially those that lay low' to be flooded. RMS suggests that a close parallel would be New Orleans slowly being engulfed after Hurricane Katrina in 2005.

Poorly maintained sea defences may have exacerbated things in some places, perhaps especially in the Somerset Levels where the former monastic management structures had broken down since the Dissolution. *Newes Out of Summerset-shire* describes:

> The sea ... meeting with land flows, strove so violently together that bearing down all things it was built to withstand and hinder the force of them, the banks were eaten through and a rupture made into Somerset. No sooner was this furious invader entered but he got up high and into the land and, encountering the River Severn, they both boiled in such pride that many miles (to the quantity of twenty in length, and four or five at least in breadth) were in a short time swallowed up in this torrent. This inundation began in the morning and, within a few hours, covered the face of the earth thereabouts to the depth of eleven or twelve feet in some places, in others more.

The sea defences may have been in a poor state of repair in some places but this would not have been the case everywhere. The tide was undoubtedly exceptionally high but this on its own would not have been enough. There were strong winds but these do not seem to have been responsible for significant damage. Was the combination of all these unprecedented? Was it, after all, a cataclysmic earthquake, more powerful than anything before or since yet which somehow left no trace elsewhere?

Or was it indeed true that, like the inhabitants of Sodom and Gomorrah or Noah's fellow men, the people living around the Bristol Channel were so irredeemably sinful that God felt he had no choice but to send them to a watery grave?

In which case, could it happen again and what would be the consequences?

6

MAJOR FLOOD EVENTS SINCE 1607

Many of the places flooded in 1607, particularly the Somerset Levels, Bristol and parts of Gloucestershire, have continued to suffer from severe floods in later years. This is largely dictated by geography. Areas at or even below sea level and flood plains of rivers will always be vulnerable, hence the increasing difficulty householders in these places are experiencing in getting affordable insurance. The event in 1607 is unique, though, in being possibly the result of a tsunami. All the other instances have been related to bad weather.

Most comparable in its suddenness and widespread effects is probably the 'Great Storm' of 1703 which occurred on 26–27 November (old style) or 7–8 December in the modern calendar. It was well-documented by observers at the time. The meteorologist William Derham recorded a low of 973 millibars in Essex and this probably deepened to 950 mb in parts of the Midlands. The whole of southern England, from the West Country to London and Kent, was affected by the storm. British naval ships returning from action in the War of the Spanish Succession, were wrecked at various locations along the Channel coast, such as Pevensey in Sussex and the Goodwin Sands, and 1,500 sailors lost their lives. Merchant shipping was damaged in the Pool of London (which should have been relatively sheltered). Part of the lead roof was blown off Westminster Abbey and at St James's Palace, Queen Anne had to seek shelter in the cellars. The first Eddystone Lighthouse was demolished and six occupants died, including its builder Henry Winstanley.

In the west, areas that had suffered in 1607 were hit once again. Hundreds of people, along with thousands of animals, drowned on the Somerset Levels. One vessel was said to have been carried fifteen miles inland. At Wells Cathedral, the bishop, Richard Kidder, was killed when two chimneys on the Bishop's Palace were brought down on him and his wife who were asleep in bed. Part of the west window of the cathedral was blown in, and at Llandaff Cathedral there was major damage to the south-west tower.

Daniel Defoe produced his first book *The Storm* in response to the calamity, which was published the following year. He wrote: 'The tempest destroyed woods and forests all over England', and that coastal towns such as Portsmouth 'looked as if the enemy had sacked them'. The Fleet was 'most miserably torn to pieces' and saw its destruction as just punishment for the navy's poor performance against the Catholic powers in the war. As in 1607 many believed the tempest represented the anger of God brought on by 'the crying sins of this nation.' In 1704, January 19 was observed as a national day of penance and fasting with leaders of Church and State calling for 'the deepest and most solemn humiliation of our people' – a demand that may not have gone down too well with ordinary folk who had suffered loss or damage to their property in the storm.

The historic centre of Bristol suffered bad flooding several times, notably in 1738, 1809, 1879 and 1896. The 1896 flooding occurred on 7–8 October and was due to a combination of a strong south-westerly wind and a period of very heavy rain. Gloucester suffered badly in 1770, 1852 and 1947 and, as in Bristol, it was usually the same parts of the city that were affected. The winter in 1947 will still be remembered by many all over the country as a particularly harsh one, and in 1952 the Lynmouth flood disaster, caused by exceptionally high rainfall over Exmoor, resulted in thirty-four deaths. Appledore, like Bristol, saw bad flooding in 1896 when a fishing boat was able to sail along Market Street. Irsha Street, where houses had been demolished by the wave in 1607, had seen a similar thing happen in 1851 when two houses were demolished by a heavy swell.

Vulnerable areas on the Welsh side of the estuary have also encountered floods since 1607. In 1792, heavy rain and floodwaters caused the bridge over the River Taff in Cardiff to collapse, severely disrupting trade; the mail coach from London had to be diverted via Llandaff. The replacement bridge was not completed until 1796. More flooding in Cardiff in 1927 caused Victoria Park Lake at Canton to overflow, leading to the escape of

Irsha Street, Appledore.

Billy the Seal, one of the park's main attractions. A song written about this escapade some time later claimed that Billy had boarded a tram in Cowbridge Road and patronised several fish and chip shops. More seriously, residents in the area had to put up with frequent flooding for many more years until a flood defence scheme was completed. The River Ely was polluted with sewage and industrial effluent until the opening of treatment works in the 1980s.

By far the worst flood disaster affected the coastal lowlands bordering the North Sea on the night of 31 January 1953. A combination of a high spring tide and strong winds caused a storm surge, bringing the water level up to over 18 feet (5.6 metres) above mean sea level. The parallels with the 1607 flood, if it was caused by a similar surge up the Bristol Channel, are significant. Sea defences were overwhelmed and the waters rushed over the unprotected flatlands behind them. In the Netherlands, 1,836 people (mainly in the province of Zeeland) died as a result of the flooding – one of these was a baby, born that night, who drowned; 307 in England (Lincolnshire, Norfolk, Suffolk and Essex – particularly Canvey Island) and 28 in Belgium (Western Flanders). In the same storm a ferry, the *Princess Victoria*, was lost at sea east of Belfast, with 133 fatalities.

Sea defences, Sandilands, Sutton-on-Sea, Lincolnshire.

The following day the Queen, who had been at Sandringham, visited Hunstanton, one of the worst-affected towns. Thirty-one people had died: fifteen locals and four American families from the USAF squadron based at nearby RAF Sculthorpe. A twenty-two-year-old American airman, Reis Leming, was later awarded the George Medal for his gallantry that night. As John Maiden of the Hunstanton Civic Society said when the disaster was commemorated in January 2013, 'Reis Leming heard people crying for help and wasted no time in donning an anti-exposure suit, grabbing a rubber life-raft and, on three separate journeys, rescued a total of 27 people. Not many people would have ventured out in those conditions. It was a tremendous act of courage'. It had been hoped that Mr Leming would be able to return to Hunstanton for this occasion but sadly he died at home in the U.S. in November 2012, aged eighty-one.

Pakefield, near Lowestoft, was one of the many places along the East Coast which had seen it all before. In the Suffolk volume of *The King's England* series (1941) Arthur Mee described how:

the older it grows the smaller it gets. Since the beginning of this century nearly a hundred of its houses and part of the village green have dropped into the sea, and the church, which used to be half a mile away, is now only 80 yards from the cliff. We talked to men who have ploughed and harvested fields now covered with sand and drowned at high tide.

Front and back of a postcard of Pakefield Church, near Lowestoft, Suffolk.

The villagers had had recent experience of dealing with disaster. On the night of 21 April 1941 two incendiary bombs fell on the thatched roof of the church. The roof and most of the interior furnishings were destroyed. The excellent church website (www.pakefieldchurch.com) describes how rebuilding began as soon as possible after the war and adds that 'the people of Pakefield have every reason to be proud of the fact that their church was the first in England to be rebuilt and rededicated [in 1950] after the war.' Just twelve years after the fire came the flood.

Author Hammond Innes, in his 1986 book *East Anglia,* wrote:

When you are on the coast of East Anglia, particularly in those parts where the country back of it is low-lying and protected by sea walls and dykes, or there are saltmarshes with a line of dunes between you and the sea, try looking at it with the eyes of people who have homes in the neighbourhood, with a view of the sea from their bedroom windows. So lovely on a fine day, with coastal flowers and the birds wheeling, but what would it be like if you were one of those householders and it was January 31st 1953? Picture it at night, with a gale blowing and a big sea running, and yourself in mortal terror of your life and the lives of your wife and children ... How hazardous and utterly terrifying.

The same words could also apply to those living around the Bristol Channel in 1607.

Incidentally, Innes tells us that a similar flood disaster in the Low Countries brought the first Flemish weavers to the England of King Henry I. They settled first at Worsted in Norfolk and then Norwich. They brought with them new techniques of cloth-making, combing instead of carding the wool, thus producing what is still known as worsted to this day.

Many scientists now believe that one effect of the trend for global warming will be more frequent periods of high rainfall and greater risk of flooding in vulnerable areas. These predictions seemed to have been vindicated in recent years with particularly severe incidents affecting Tewkesbury and Gloucester in 2005 and the Somerset Levels at the end of 2012, a year that began with three months of drought warnings! National government agencies and local councils are having to consider their response to the new situation.

Sheringham in Norfolk, where the soft cliffs have little resistance to erosion, is one of the places where the Environment Agency is adopting a controversial policy of 'managed retreat'. The 1953 storm wrecked Sheringham's wooden sea defences. These were replaced by a concrete sea wall, which doubles as the resort's promenade. In 1976 a system of revetments and groynes was established eastwards along the coast towards West Runton but this is no longer being maintained and is in poor repair. Sections that become hazardous will be taken down and the coastline allowed to evolve without human interference.

Beeston Hill, Sheringham.

Changing weather patterns are naturally causing great concern in the areas flooded in 1607 – though the reasons may well be different. The consequences of a similar disaster in the future will be considered later in this book but before that we take a journey along the coast from West Wales to Gloucester and round to North Devon and beyond to learn in more detail what happened in each district and what reminders of the 1607 flood can still be seen. Many of these places are still deemed to be at considerable (and possibly increasing) risk of flooding in the future.

7

GAZETTEER

This gazetteer section follows the coastline and vulnerable lowlands from West Wales round to Cornwall in geographical sequence, detailing how they were affected by the flood in 1607 and what evidence of the event can still be seen by visitors. Use of the relevant Ordnance Survey 1:50,000 *Landranger* map is recommended. Sheets 162, 171, 172, 181 and 182 cover the areas of Glamorgan, Monmouthshire, Gloucestershire and Somerset that were worst affected. For some places reference is also made to other flood events or legends or to present-day flood defence schemes. These places are also listed alphabetically in the index.

CARDIGAN BAY

As we have seen, the effects of the 1607 flood were mainly confined to the coastal lowlands on either side of the Bristol Channel. However, the '400 Year Retrospective' report by Risk Management Solutions, indicates that 'flooding also was said to have extended along the coasts of southern Wales … over Laugharne and Llanstephan in Carmarthenshire and into Cardiganshire, although there are no detailed accounts from this area'.

Cardigan Bay does though have its own flood story, the legend of Cantre'r Gwaelod, the 'Welsh Atlantis', whose details mirror those of the 1607 flood in some respects. The area between Ramsay Island and Bardsey Island was, like the Gwent Levels today, an area of low-lying land, protected from the sea by a dyke known as Sarn Badrig (St Patrick's Causeway) with a series of sluice gates which were opened at low tide to drain the land. It was said to have once extended up to twenty miles west of the present coastline and to be so fertile that an acre of it was worth as much as four acres anywhere else.

Exactly how and when this tract of land came to be flooded is unclear. The earliest known version of the legend is a poem in the *Black Book of Carmarthen* (*Llyfr Du Caerfyrddin*), from around 1250, which blames the disaster on a pagan priestess called Mererid who allegedly allowed a magical well that she was supposed to be keeping an eye on to overflow. It would appear to have been an expensive piece of negligence!

In a version of the myth which dates from the seventeenth century, two local nobles shared responsibility for the upkeep of the sea wall. One of these men, Seithenyn, described as 'a notorious drunkard and carouser', likewise neglected his duties and allowed the sea to break through the dyke and flood the whole area. Said to be a friend of the king, he fell asleep as a result of over-imbibing and failed to notice an oncoming storm. The sluices were left open and the sea rushed in, drowning sixteen villages and all the farmland. This account later did duty as a moral tale on the evils of the demon drink and much use was made of it by preachers in nonconformist chapels.

Another somewhat bawdier version combines the two tales. This maintains that Seithenyn was a visiting king who, at the time of the storm, was romancing the priestess Mererid and she was, to put it delicately, not in a position to close the sluices when the storm threatened. Doubtless the same puritanical preachers employed this variation to warn of the consequences of being distracted from duty by lust!

Whatever version takes your fancy, the legend of Cantre'r Gwaelod has inspired many poems, songs and stories from the time of the *Black Book of Carmarthen* in the thirteenth century to the present day. It was the basis of Thomas Love Peacock's 1829 novel *The Misfortunes of Elphin*. In 1920, the geologist William Ashton in his snappily titled *The Evolution of a Coastline, Barrow to Aberystwyth and the Isle of Man, with notes on Lost Towns, Submarine Discoveries Etc.* used Ptolemy's map of Great Britain and Ireland with its almost-straight west coast of Wales, as evidence that Cardigan Bay covered an area of land that had been lost since ancient times.

The folk song 'Clychau Aberdyfi' ('The Bells of Aberdovey'), which dates from the eighteenth century, is based on the detail in the story that the bells can be heard ringing beneath the waves. The song first appears in an opera, *Liberty Hall*, written by Charles Dibdin, a writer well known for his songs of the sea. The Welsh words were written by John Ceiriog Hughes in the nineteenth century. In 1936, the bells of St Peter's Church in the town were adapted to enable them to play the tune, and in 2011 a piece of artwork by sculptor Marcus Vergette was installed beneath the jetty in the harbour, the tide being harnessed to ring a bell in homage to the legend. The story has also featured in the BBC television *Coast* series. Presenter Neil Oliver visited Aberdyfi and Ynylas near Borth to examine the remains of the submerged forest and Sarn Badrig which are exposed at low tide. These were the subject of an underwater exploration undertaken by the conservation group Friends of Cardigan Bay in 2006.

It is from these fragmentary remains that the legend of Cantre'r Gwaelod is believed to have been derived. The remains of oak, pine, birch and willow that have been preserved by the acid anaerobic soil conditions are estimated to be 5,000 years old. In 1770 the Welsh antiquarian William Owen Pughe described seeing remains of buildings about four miles off the coast between the mouths of the Ystwyth and Teifi rivers. Samuel Lewis's 1846 *Topographical Dictionary of Wales* described stone walls and causeways beneath the shallow waters of Cardigan Bay. These can still be seen today, a series of ridges (called Sarnau) at right-angles to the coast and stretching for several miles. However, sadly for lovers of Welsh legends, modern geologists believe that they are glacial moraines dating from the end of the last Ice Age.

The harbour at Aberdovey.

Clarach Bay, Aberystwyth.

The Legend of Cantre'r Gwaelod is probably just one of the inundation myths that are found in cultures all over the world, Noah's Flood included. Basil Cracknell, in *Outrageous Waves: Global Warming and Coastal Change in Britain*, refers also to the Irish saga of Branwen, written down as early as 1100, which seems to be based on a memory of the time when the Irish Sea was encroaching on the land. He quotes the line: 'Afterwards the ocean spread out, at the time when the ocean conquered the kingdoms.' These may be folk memories of the inundations that followed the melting of the glaciers at the end of the Ice Age. He adds that 'there is no doubt that submergence has taken place and that a low-lying boulder clay area once extended some distance seawards from the present coastline.' This event, however, took place at some unknown date before historical records, and knowledge of it survives only partially in legends and sagas. It would have involved a rise in sea level in relation to the land of some 60 feet (about 20 metres) and would have had a dramatic effect on the coastline of the rest of the British Isles. Cracknell suggests that 'it is perhaps significant that both the time when these stories were first written down and the one to which they are supposed to relate (*c.* AD 500) were periods of rising sea level'. There is however no evidence of anything so dramatic happening recently enough to be described by eyewitnesses.

The 1607 flood, by contrast, is well-documented and there is plenty of physical evidence to be seen as we follow the Bristol Channel coastline.

CARMARTHEN BAY

The attractive little town of Laugharne is best known for its associations with Dylan Thomas but has a long history. The church contains a small pre-Norman cross, and the castle remains that are now visible date from a thirteenth-century rebuilding. It was mentioned at the time as being one of the places affected by the 1607 flood but how badly it was affected is not known. Historians believe that the flood may have contributed to the silting up of the harbour, which in earlier times had been a prosperous port.

John Saxton's 1607 map of Carmarthenshire showed two separate place names near Kidwelly, known as Llansaint and Hawton, or Hawtenchurch, where there was subsequently only one village – Llansaint. This led to the suggestion that Hawton had been destroyed in the Great Flood. However, according to the journal *Carmarthen Antiquary* in 2003, research by the late Professor Stephens, who lived nearby at Ferryside, showed that its name was simply the English version of the Welsh Llansaint ('Church of the Saints' or 'All Saints') and that there was only ever one village.

Remains of medieval fish-weirs, belonging to Carmarthen or Whitland Priories, have been found in the vicinity of Kidwelly, perhaps giving credence to the idea that a village had been destroyed in 1607, but it seems likely that the shifting nature of the dunes on this stretch of coast means that, in any event, it has changed out of all recognition in the last 400 years.

One of the contemporary pamphlets records that:

> There was in the county of Carmarthen a young woman who had four small children and not one of them able to save itself. The mother, seeing the furies of the waters to be so violent to seize upon her, threatening the destruction of herself and her small children, as a woman's wit is ever ready in such extremities, took a long trough wherein she placed herself and her children. And so, putting themselves to the mercies of the waters, they were all by that means driven to the dry land and by God's good providence thereby they were all saved.

Possibly this West Wales family would not have been too impressed by the fact that the pamphlet in question was titled *God's Warning to his people of England*!

GLAMORGAN COAST – MUMBLES TO OGMORE

The coastline of Glamorgan has also seen encroachment by the sea in the relatively recent past, although this cannot be directly related to the 1607 event. The sea has certainly advanced in the areas between the Mumbles near Swansea to the mouth of the Ogmore near Bridgend. According to the historian Chris Barber in *Mysterious Wales*, the shores of Swansea Bay were formerly between three and five miles (about 5km) further out than at present. He states that 'fishermen have claimed that over the area known as Green Grounds they have sometimes seen the foundations of ancient homesteads, overwhelmed by a terrific storm which raged long ago'.

He refers to stories of an extensive forest, Coed Aran ('Silver Wood') – now submerged – that stretched from Mumbles to Kenfig Burrows and of a long-lost bridle path from Penrice Castle to Margam Abbey near Port Talbot.

The name of Kenfig, near Porthcawl, is believed to be a corruption of the Welsh Cefn-y-figen, the high ground above the marsh. Kenfig is about a mile from the present coastline and there is a legend concerning a tremendous flood caused by an incursion of the sea during a violent storm in the Bristol Channel in the mid-sixteenth century. The antiquarian and traveller Leland in 1540 described the ruins of the settlement and castle, saying that they had been almost completely buried by drifting sand.

This was not the first time such a thing had happened. In *Outrageous Waves* Basil Cracknell records that 'between September 1314 and April 1316 great storms pushed the sand dunes over half the pasture called "conyger" near Kenfig.' Rents were reduced because of the damage done and at Neath meadows were said to have become 'worth nothing'.

The pamphlet *God's Warning* records a number of lucky escapes from the waves, stating that:

> There was in the county of Glamorgan a man both blind and did ride [to safety?] and one which had not been able to stand upon his legs in ten years before. He had his poor cottage broken down by the force of the waters and himself, bed and all carried into the open fields where, being ready to sink and at a point to seek a resting place, two fathoms deep under the waters, his hand by chance caught hold of the rafter of a house swimming by the fierceness of the winds then blowing easterly, he was driven to dry land and so saved … In another place there was a child of the age of five or six years which was kept swimming for the space of two hours by the reason that his

View across Swansea Bay.

long coat lay spread upon the tops of the waters. Being at last at the very point to sink, there came by chance, floating upon the water, a fat wether that was dead, very full of wool. The poor distressed child, perceiving this good means of recovery, caught fast hold on the wether's wool and likewise, with the wind, he was driven to dry land and so saved.

CARDIFF

William Rees, in his definitive *Cardiff – a History of the City* (1969), describes how the 1607 flood hastened the abandonment of St Mary's, the Mother Church of Cardiff. Situated on vulnerable low-lying land in a bend of the River Taff, the building was inundated, resulting in serious damage to the fabric. *God's Warning* states that 'in Cardiff … there was a great part of the church next the water beaten down. Many houses and gardens there, which were near the water side, were all overflowed and much harm done'.

Rees quotes John Speed, whose map of Cardiff was published in 1610, who, as previously stated, described the Taff as 'a foe of St Marie's Church, with undermining her foundations and threatening her fall'. His plan shows that by 1610 a corner of the churchyard had been swept away. Services continued to be held in St Mary's until the middle of the century but the burghers of Cardiff preferred to spend whatever funds were available on St John's, which stood on higher ground away from the river. By 1678, St Mary's was a roofless ruin and its tower had fallen. The antiquarian Edward Lloyd stated at that time that the church had been further damaged during the Civil War and that little more than its east wall remained. He went on to say that 'the Taff had encroached so far into the churchyard as to run close by it', and that the only burials in the churchyard were of those people 'who wish to be buried beside their ancestors'. The more-securely located St John's took on its civic functions. Nevertheless, burials continued at St Mary's until 1707 and children were baptised in the ruined building as late as the 1730s.

A letter to the *South Wales Daily News* in 1907, quoted by Dennis Morgan, recalled that sixty years earlier 'there were frequently to be seen portions of human skeletons exposed when a heavy flood washed off some of the river bank' by the old churchyard. In the 1850s, the Taff was diverted away from the former site of St Mary's to facilitate the construction of Brunel's South Wales Railway and what became Cardiff General railway station.

The present St Mary's in Bute Road is on an entirely different site. As the population of Butetown expanded, the second Marquis of Bute encouraged the idea of rebuilding St Mary's there, and provided a site in Bute Road and £1,000 towards the cost of the project. The Poet Laureate, William Wordsworth, even contributed a poem in support of the scheme. The original site of St Mary's was not forgotten and is marked by the outline in the side of the pub at the corner of Wood Street and St Mary's Street, close to the bus station.

The 1607 disaster did not only affect the town centre. *Woeful News from Wales* described how it was:

> 24 miles in length and more than four miles in breadth … so that even on higher ground at Llandaff, where Mistress Matthews lost 400 sheep, no-one was spared from the woeful impact of the deluge … Mistress Van of Llandaff, a gentlewoman of good sort saw the flood approaching but was overwhelmed by the surging swell before she could reach an upper room in her house.

Dennis Morgan, in his *Illustrated History of Cardiff Suburbs* (2003), states that 'the whole of Cardiff was flooded but it was the low-lying parishes to the east of the borough that suffered most'. This, sadly, was not a new experience for Cardiff. The town was constantly at risk from rising waters. Floods in 1550 and 1578 had caused considerable damage and there were further inundations in 1703, 1763, 1775 and 1791. In a footnote, Rees describes how in 1763 a Spring tide 'enveloped the Moors at Canton, drowning many sheep and breaking over the sea wall'. The 1791 flood caused severe damage to houses alongside the Taff so that 'scarcely any houses survived on the bank of the river … St Mary's Street was almost a one-sided street, the houses and all traces of the old town wall on this side having been swept away.'

Rumney

Beyond the superstores on the edge of the city, the road from Cardiff towards Newport climbs a steep hill up to Rumney and runs along a prominent ridge with views on both sides. The tower of the parish church can be seen, somewhat below the roofs of the houses and shops, on the downslope towards the coastline. In 1607, somewhere along this stretch of sea wall bodies were washed up, and were buried in a communal grave near the church.

Mardy Road, Wentloog Levels.

Newman, in *The Buildings of Wales – Glamorgan,* describes Rumney as 'a featureless outer suburb where the medieval church is an unexpected find'. St Augustine's certainly looks like an ancient village church and is situated in quiet residential streets but, sadly, was locked when I visited.

These streets lead down to Wentloog Road and the Levels. If you cross the railway bridge in Mardy Road you come to an area of small factories. Mardy Road then turns off to the right and becomes a rural lane, seemingly little changed over the centuries. It leads to a caravan park and a section of the medieval sea wall at Mardy Farm. This is now a listed ancient monument, monitored by the Glamorgan and Gwent Archaeological Trust.

In February 1590/1 the Court of Augmentations noted that 'the Manor of Rumney lies adjoining the sea. There is a wall between the sea and lordship for the defence of the same, which wall being about two years past in great decay was by commission new made and placed more into the land than before it was.'

If you retrace your steps back to the main road – where the drivers of lorries and vans seem determined to make the most of the apparent lack of speed limits – and turn right, you come to the entrance to a modern business park.

Prominent boards advertise the availability of new units to rent or buy. We are well onto the Levels now and I trust that any businessman taking on one of these units makes sure he has good flood insurance!

Heavy lorries were rumbling down Newton Lane, probably heading for the recycling site, so I did not venture down it. Had I done so, I would have come to Newton, believed to be the site of the house belonging in 1607 to John Dunne.

The Gwent Levels – Wentloog

The Wentloog Levels, west of the mouth of the River Usk, with the Caldicot Levels to the east of it, together known as the Gwent Levels, was one of the areas worst affected in 1607. Still possessing an evocative and distinctive landscape, the area preserves, particularly in its churches, contemporary memorials to the disaster. Much of our knowledge of the district in the past derives from Archdeacon William Coxe's monumental *Historical Tour Through Monmouthshire*, published in 1801 and based on his travels through the county at the end of the eighteenth century. Archdeacon William Coxe was one of the learned clergyman of that period whose pastoral duties were apparently light enough to allow them plenty of time for antiquarian research. His evocative description of the landscape (though not perhaps the people) of the Levels still holds good today:

> We next visited the three churches of the Level, St Bride's, Peterstone and Marshfield. The ground, like marshy plains which have been drained, is cut into parallel ditches, in some of which the water stagnates, in others it runs in perpetual streams, called reens, which fall into the sea through flood gates or gouts. The roads leading through these flat marshes are straight and narrow and exhaust the patience of the traveller. The marshes, being only inhabited by farmers and labourers, contain very few houses and cottages. The natives are in general Welsh and many of them scarcely understand English; consequently the churches are served in the Welsh language. In former times the population must have been considerable, because the churches are large and capable of containing great congregations, though now reduced to forty or fifty persons.

Coxe's comments on the small population and large churches are very significant. It was nearly two centuries after the Levels were devastated in the 1607 flood and the population had clearly not recovered. As we shall see at Porton, on the Caldicot Levels, the majority of the cottages that were there at the time of the flood would not have survived.

Arthur Mee in his 1951 book *The King's England: Monmouthshire* also captured the distinct character of the Levels, which he said were:

> in curious contrast to the urban areas of Newport and Cardiff which immediately adjoin them. Here is an area of nearly 25,000 acres stretching 20 miles along the coast and three miles inland, much of it below the high-water mark ... The soil is mainly bluish marsh clay deposited by the tide which formerly reached the old cliff line, traceable behind the levels. Mixed with the clay is sand and gravel brought down by the Usk and Rhymney ... Almost all the area is under grass, producing meat and milk, and nearly every farm has a little cider orchard. The villages are not of the scattered upland type, for the houses are usually clustered together round the church. Not only has the protective sea wall made all this possible, but it has provided an unexpected additional benefit: mud has silted against its outer edge, forming a narrow strip of salt marsh suitable for grazing young cattle at low tide.

Basil Cracknell, in *Outrageous Waves*, says of the Gwent Levels that they are of particular interest because their exploitation depended on the building of sea walls. Unlike the Fens or Romney Marsh, there are no shingle beaches or clay belt at the coast to protect the marshes from the sea. 'It is in this region,' he writes, 'that we have the first definite evidence that the Romans built the earliest sea walls in Britain. Elsewhere it is a matter of speculation.'

Archaeological evidence shows that the Romans were the first to construct a sea wall and drain the Levels. 'The main ditches were also probably cut by the Romans,' Arthur Mee wrote. 'The reens are up to six feet deep and the villagers jump across them with long poles.' (Whether this last statement is still true I am unable to say. I have certainly never seen it done but when we moved from Middlesex to Redwick, on the Caldicot Levels, we were told that you were not considered truly a local until you had ended up in a reen!)

If the Gwent Levels are, in Cracknell's words, of 'a remarkable testimony to the lasting effectiveness of the Romans' achievements', the role of the monasteries in the middle ages was also crucial. The abbeys at Margam and

Tintern were both important landowners on the levels and were prepared to make significant investment in sea defences and drainage schemes to improve the value of their holdings. Stephen Rippon's *The Severn Estuary: Landscape Evolution and Wetlands Reclamation* (1997) describes the evolution of the landscape in this area in far greater detail than I can here.

St Brides, Wentloog

Coxe wrote that:

> The tower is a handsome structure of hewn stone in the gothic style of architecture and more modern than the other parts, which are of coarser materials … On the south wall of the church, within a porch which forms the principal entrance, is an inscription carved in freestone:

TE. GREAT. FLVD

20 IANVARIE

IN TE MORNING

1606

Flood plaque in porch, St Brides, Wentloog Church.

The lower part of this inscription, which marks the height to which the waters arrived, is about five feet from the ground. A second inundation in 1708 covered the Level from Magor to Cardiff and another happened a few years ago, but neither was so high as that of 1606.

Peterstone

Coxe described a church once grand but now in poor condition:

> The church of Peterstone, situated at a distance of six miles to the south-west of St Bride's and within a quarter of a mile from the sea walls, is a singularly large and elegant edifice for a district so remote and ill-habited … the church is greatly dilapidated … the arches are bulged and the columns have considerably declined from the perpendicular direction.

Bradney, in his *History of Monmouthshire* (vol. 5, edited by Madeleine Gray, 1993), stated that the church was built on piles to raise it above sea level and adds that 'there are no graves because of the floods and therefore no monumental inscriptions.'

A stone in the outside wall of the chancel marked the water level of the 1607 flood. Sadly, although the church was later restored from the parlous state in which Coxe saw it, it has more recently become redundant and converted into a private house and there is consequently no public access.

Peterstone has had a chequered relationship with the waters of the estuary. Arthur Mee wrote: 'In its day this small village on the Wentloog Level was a flourishing seaport, even rivalling Cardiff. Unhappily Peterstone Great Wharf, which now keeps out the Severn, became sadly neglected and the sea came through. Now nothing remains of the port but the boundary banks of a dock.'

Marshfield, the third church visited by Archdeacon Coxe on his tour of the Wentloog Levels, has a pleasant rural setting in an area that has largely become suburbanized by the proximity of Cardiff and Newport, and much of architectural interest, but no relics of the flood.

NEWPORT

Newport stands a few miles back from the coast and is a surprisingly hilly place. Much of the modern town and also the district around the ancient church, now St Woolos Cathedral, is well above any flood risk. However, there are low-lying areas, still considered to be in danger of inundation, close to the River Usk below the City Centre and down to the mouth of the river.

There do not appear to be any references in contemporary documents to flooding in the town in 1607, but this inconvenient fact did not deter its historians from writing some imaginative accounts of what might have happened. James Matthews, in *Historic Newport*, first published in 1910 (reprinted 1996), writes:

> The marshes within the confines of Crindau Pill were nothing better than a swamp and formed an island near the Mill; the marshes from the Town Pill to Pillgwenlly were a water-soaked fen, a veritable quagmire. The Town Pill ran up to the present Bryngwyn Road, making Stow Hill a peninsula and the sea came up nearly to Bassaleg Church.

In recent years a massive new Sainsbury's store has been built on the low-lying land by Crindau Pill. It has excellent road access from the M4 and A4042 into Newport but looks very vulnerable to flooding. South of the Town Bridge there are modern developments completed or in the planning stage on both sides of the river and one hopes that due attention has been paid to flood defences as without them these areas can no longer fulfil their former role as flood plains.

Matthews also describes the events of September 1829 when 'several thousand pounds worth of damage was done by the high tides of the 14th and 15th by overflowing several wharves and quay walls which gave way as the tide receded, precipitating several hundred tons of iron into the water'.

Haydn Davis, in his 1998 *History of the Borough of Newport*, also tends to the dramatic. He goes on to describe how, in 1607:

> [the waters] driven by storm-force winds, quickly breached what passed for coastal defence works at several points and covered the whole of the moors from Caldicot to Cardiff in a surging spate. What effect this inundation had on the town, is not recorded but it does not take much imagination to picture the consternation of the townsfolk as, within sight of the West Gate, large waves rolled across the Pillgwenlly marshes. It has been written that at its height the flood lapped at the edge of Bassaleg Churchyard and, this being so, it must have washed through the ground floor of Tredegar House.

Bassaleg Church, near Newport.

The Tredegar House mentioned would have been the older structure praised by Leland in 1540 as 'a very fair house'. Parts of this survive within the mansion built by the Morgan family in the second half of the seventeenth century and now in the care of the National Trust. Pillgwenlly, now a busy multicultural district south of the City Centre became built up in the late nineteenth and early twentieth century as Newport's docks and steel industries grew rapidly. Bassaleg (pronounced 'Baze-leg') Church still stands on high ground overlooking the Ebbw River in Newport's western suburbs.

THE GWENT LEVELS – CALDICOT

In *The Making of Wales*, historian John Davies describes the Gwent Levels as 'Wales's most remarkable example of labour-intensive landscape management'. The history of drainage and land management on the Levels began with the Romans, with the sea wall at Goldcliff constructed by the garrison from Caerleon. The network of channels was maintained throughout the Middle Ages – the tenants of the Lord of Gwynllwg drained the Wentloog Levels to the west of the Usk (*see* pp 58-9) and monks from Tintern Abbey did the same on the eastern side. The name of the Monks Ditch, one of the major drainage channels, best seen at Whitson, still recalls the monastic influence on the landscape. Controlled flooding of meadowland to improve the grazing was a common practice, done by using stone sluices which could be blocked with wooden planks. The distinctive settlement plan of Whitson reflects later reclamation, some suggest by Dutch settlers. John Newman describes Whitson as 'one of the most evocative places on the Gwent Levels. Set back to the east of the road is what amounts to a row of substantial eighteenth century farmhouses, suggesting vividly the richness of the meadowlands drained by a network of willow-lined ditches'.

The Levels are registered as a Landscape of Outstanding Historic Interest in Wales, and an SSSI (Site of Special Scientific Interest), important statutory protection in an area of the M4 corridor where the political and economic pressures in favour of infrastructure development (which could be disastrous) are very strong – but it is an area of unique environmental

Levels landscape near Whitson.

importance and historical significance. The path along the sea wall eastwards from Nash and Goldcliff gives extensive views across the historic levels landscape and across to the Somerset coast.

'Eventually,' wrote John Davies, 'the Gwent Levels would have 40 miles of wide ditches, 85 miles of narrow ditches and 750 miles of gutters.' These different artificial watercourses had their own distinctive local names that are still familiar to local people to this day: 'reens' collect all the water off the fields and lead it off towards the sea; 'grips' are small hand-dug ditches while 'gouts' are the sluices which regulate the flow of water into the sea, depending on the state of the tide. The existence of these systems, even though they could not prevent the disaster of 1607, did at least enable farming in the area to recover in the years that followed.

Archdeacon Coxe, writing in about 1800, described how:

> the dykes or walls extend from Caldicot almost the whole way to Goldcliff. They were formerly mounds of earth but, being subject to frequent dilapidation and consequently incurring the expense of continual repairs, have been recently constructed with stone. These extensive dykes are kept in repair by the contributions of the proprietors of Caldicot Level, according to their respective proportions. The laws by which the expense is regulated are similar to the ordinances of Henry de Bathe, a famous justice itinerant who, in the reign of Henry III was commissioned to inquire into and regulate the proportions to be paid by the proprietors of Romney Marsh in Kent. From these ordinances the whole realm of England takes directions in relation to the commissioners of sewers and to the jurors for regulating the expense of securing, rearing and maintaining these artificial bounds to the ravages of the sea.

The modern successor to Henry's Commissioners of Sewers in this area is the Caldicot and Wentloog Levels Internal Drainage Board, whose responsibilities to protect the land from the ravages of the sea remain the same. Its board includes specialist engineers, local councillors and eighteen members elected from among the landowners who pay rates to the organisation. It is financed mainly from levies raised from Monmouthshire, Newport and Cardiff councils.

In June 2008 the Environment Agency announced plans to invest around £70 million in a new flood defence scheme for the Gwent Levels, with a higher priority being given to residential areas compared to farmland. This prioritisation was, unsurprisingly, not appreciated by the farming community. Len Attewell, whose farm lay next to sea defences at Undy, told the *South Wales Argus* that 'if cropland was flooded for any length of time, the salt in the seawater would render the land useless for farming'. Monmouth MP David Davies blamed Labour government cuts in funding to the Environment Agency for the risk to farmland. 'In this period of rocketing food prices,' he said, 'prime agricultural land along the Gwent Levels should be as important to protect as people and their homes.' However, local residents, such as the inhabitants of the Lighthouse Park estate in St Brides, who had been evacuated from their homes in floods earlier in the year, welcomed the plans.

Nash

To get a feeling for what the landscape of the Levels must have been like before reclamation – and what it might become again if the worst happens – it is worth visiting the Newport Wetland Centre at Nash. Over a thousand acres of land was deliberately flooded to create a wildlife habitat to compensate for the loss of a similar wetland area due to the controversial Cardiff Bay Barrage Scheme. Much of the area flooded in what some saw as a cynical trade-off was a former fuel oil disposal site but some farmland in the parishes of Nash and Goldcliff was also lost. However, the nature reserve that was established there in 2000 soon proved to be a popular visitor attraction.

The landscape is a surreal contrast between the wide views across the reed-beds to the Severn Estuary and the massive pylons, Uskmouth Power Stations and distant glimpses of industrial Newport following the River Usk. A barrage has been proposed for the Usk as well and planning permission has recently been granted for exploratory oil-drilling on a site adjacent to the wetlands.

In the distance is the fourteenth-century spire of St Mary's Church. Several feet off the ground on one of the buttresses of the tower is a marker showing the level reached by the 1607 flood. The church's unspoilt Georgian interior, with high-backed box pews, three-decker pulpit and west gallery, is also of great interest. In *The Buildings of Wales – Gwent/ Monmouthshire* John Newman describes St Mary's as 'an extraordinary surprise, standing alone but for a scatter of council houses in the flat meadows on the outskirts of Newport'. He adds that 'the steeple was built by Eton College, holders of the rectory of Nash since 1450.' When news

Nash Church, believed to be pictured in the woodcut. The flood mark is on the base of the tower.

of the flood disaster in Monmouthshire finally reached Eton it must have caused some concern to the authorities at the college, worried for the value of their landholdings.

Goldcliff, Whitson and Porton

Goldcliff, sometimes spelled with a final e, is – according to the *Newport Coast Path* guidebook – named after a limestone cliff, about sixty feet high, that once rose over a great bed of yellow mica that had a glittering appearance in sunshine, especially from ships in the Bristol Channel. In 1878, a stone with a worn inscription was found near the base of the sea wall here. Now in the Roman museum at Caerleon, it reads (in translation from the Latin): 'The Century of Statorius Maximus in the First Cohort built thirty-one and a half paces.' It suggests that the legion's landholding extended all the way to Goldcliff from Caerleon and was worth a great deal of effort to protect from the sea.

The link with Caerleon was long-lasting. In 1113, a Benedictine priory was founded at Goldcliff by Robert de Chandos, Lord of Caerleon, under a charter from Henry I, for a prior and twelve monks. There is nothing left to see now. Its site was on the high point of the so-called 'gold cliff', facing the

The flood brass in Goldcliff Church.

Severn estuary. It seems that latterly the monks were not all as moral as they should have been. By the end of the thirteenth century the monks were doing well financially. They had the right of shipping goods free of harbour dues into the ports of Bristol, Newport and Cardiff. Being in charge of this lucrative enterprise must have been a tempting prospect because in 1332 one William Martel, a monk from Tintern Abbey, became the Prior, having forged a document from the Pope and engineered the removal of Prior Philip. His crime was uncovered and Philip was reinstated by Edward III. However, he also proved to be something of a bad lot because a few years later, Philip, along with twenty others, three of them priests, was indicted for looting barrels of wine and other goods from a ship wrecked nearby.

Perhaps it was a judgement that in 1424 the priory was partly destroyed by a flood. The last monks left in 1467, and in the years that followed – and following the Reformation – the remaining priory buildings were swept away by the sea. Paul Courtney, in *The Gwent County History, Vol. 3* (edited by Madeleine Gray and Prys Morgan), writes:

> In 1504 the patent rolls record the appointment of a commission of sewers to deal with the flooding of Goldcliff marsh ..... in 1520 a private action by Anthony Walsh was taken in the court of Chancery against the Provost of Eton who had apparently allowed the middle ditch in his manor of Goldcliff to be left unscoured, causing flooding in Llanwern.

Courtney also tells us that:

> The agricultural writer Charles Hassall noted in 1812 that the sea walls of the Caldicot Level were superior to those on the Wentloog Level. The former apparently had stone facings on the side facing the sea and also often on the inland side. Hassall further recorded that the system was defective between Llanwern and Whitson, giving rise to the 'rushy and coarse' state of the ground. William Coxe commented in 1801 that Goldcliff's walls had only recently been rebuilt with stone facings.

The little church at Goldcliff was built following the damage to the priory in 1424. Its south and west walls are built of squared limestone blocks possibly salvaged from the priory. However, some of the original fabric of the building appears to be older. Rippon, in the Council for British Archaeology's report *The Gwent Levels – the Evolution of the Landscape* (1996), suggests that the church may even be an early barn conversion. Whatever its origins, Goldcliff Church is home to one of the most authentic and evocative memorials to the Great Flood. A small contemporary brass plaque in the north wall of the sanctuary reads – in attempted verse form – '1606 - On the XX day of Ianuary even as it came to pas / it pleased God the flud did flow to the edge of this same bras / and in this parish theare was lost 5000 and od powndes / besides XXII people was in this parrish drownd / Goldclif John Wilkins of Pil Rew and William Tap Church Wardens 1609.' Perhaps it says something about the Churchwardens' priorities that the loss of property gets mentioned before the loss of life (although it may be more to do with creating a satisfactory rhyme!)

Goldcliff Church is quite difficult to find as it is set back and hidden from the road. It is reached down a track alongside the Farmers Arms pub (where you can park). Do not be misled by the booklet *Newport Coast Path* (2013) which gives the impression that the flood brass is in the church at Whitson.

The Royal Commission on Ancient and Historical Monuments in Wales website (www.rcahmw.gov.uk) draws attention to the fact that although stone-built churches on the Levels survived the flood, many houses did not. On this alluvial plain, lacking building stone or even much timber, it was always going to be difficult to construct anything that could resist surging floodwaters. However, at Little Porton near Goldcliff, close to the abandoned Whitson Church, is a post-flood building originally built of a building material that had probably been widely used in the area previously – 'gre', a form of sticky marine clay. The front and side walls have been rebuilt but the rear is still clay. It is a rare survival because, of course, when clay walls get wet they collapse. This would explain why no pre-1607 houses survive on the Levels.

Whitson Church (erroneously labelled as St Mary Magdalene's in the coast path guidebook) with its little leaning tower is reached along the dead-end lane to Porton. Visitors must keep to the path from the lane as the orchard it runs across is private property. The church itself has been scandalously left to deteriorate and is in a dangerous condition.

Redwick (Monmouthshire)

Arthur Mee waxes lyrical about Redwick. Writing in *The King's England: Monmouthshire* in 1951, he describes: 'The church stands serenely at its heart, as it has for 600 years or more; and all around it, scattered far and wide, are cottages in gardens fair to look on.' John Newman (2000) is less romantic but more precise: 'The church stands at the centre of a loosely nucleated village.'

Most of Redwick's houses are comparatively modern and spread along South Row and Bryn Road which loop either side of Church Row. There are quite big gaps between the houses and the population of the village today is under 200 people, yet Redwick's church is sturdy and medieval: 'One of the finest of among the churches of the Levels,' according to Newman. The 1607 flood may be significant in seeking an explanation for this anomaly. As shown in the RCAHMW report on Little Porton, a likely building material for pre-flood houses on the Levels is clay and these would not have survived a major flood. Is it possible that pre-1607 Redwick was a larger and more important place than it is now? Do the gaps between the houses today mark plots where lost buildings were never rebuilt?

The second Redwick mystery concerns the flood marks on the church, for Redwick has two, at slightly different heights. One is on the south-east corner of the chancel, seen as visitors approach the church from the main gate by the former school-house; the other is to the right of the entrance to the porch. The two marks were the subject of an investigation carried out by the South East Wales Young Archaeologists Club, led by Mark Lewis, and reported in the 2007 volume of *The Monmouthshire Antiquary*. Lewis comes to the conclusion that the one on the corner of the building was the genuine one, and that the more obvious one on the porch was added 'during or soon after the restoration of the church in 1875' and the level taken from the adjacent medieval mass dial scratched onto the stonework. The brass plate, set between the stones of the porch and pictured in the *Newport Coast Path* guide, was, according to Mark Lewis, 'probably added between 1954 and 1979 by Redwick resident Hubert Jones, an antiquarian whose legacy is found throughout the parish to this day'. Among other things, Mr Jones was responsible for what Newman describes as 'an Arts & Crafts-style Cider Press and Bus Shelter, built of stone and concrete as late as c.1975', which houses cider-making equipment, mill stones and other relics of local historical significance. BBC Wales' Derek Brockway described this distinctive structure as 'a hobbit house built by a local eccentric' in his *Weatherman Walking* television series.

Other features of Redwick Church include a total immersion font, rare in an Anglican setting, and the mutilated remains of what must once have been a fine medieval screen. This was badly damaged in 1942 when Redwick became the unlikely target for a German bomber. Four high-explosive bombs were dropped nearby, destroying one cottage completely

Flood mark on the corner of the exterior of Redwick church.

and damaging the church and schoolhouse. Some have claimed since that this accounts for the slightly alarming leaning of the ancient church tower. Lewis, however, is categorical in stating that the tower 'long ago settled into the alluvium', a fact that he said would 'be a relief to the Church Council'. The people of Redwick are certainly well aware of their village's history. In 2007 the church was the focus of a year-long programme of events to mark the 400th anniversary of the flood, and in 2012 a special service and exhibition of memorabilia were held to commemorate the bombing.

CHEPSTOW TO GLOUCESTER

Chepstow

Chepstow is where the River Wye enters the Severn and is a good place to see just how big the tidal range in the estuary is, even under normal conditions. From both the castle and the town bridge, extensive areas of mud can be seen exposed at low tide and the dark stain on the cliffs on the English side shows the level of high tides.

In 1607, Chepstow's bridge would have been constructed of wood but its subsequent history was quite complicated. The town's museum shows its development in a fascinating series of pictures. There is a scale model made in 1969 which shows the bridge with stone piers on the Monmouthshire side, but wooden ones still on Gloucestershire's. This was how it appeared between 1784 and 1814 when work began on a cast-iron structure.

The elegant iron lattice arched bridge that we see today was built to the designs of John Rennie and opened in 1816 and replaced the historic structure seen by Archdeacon Coxe less than twenty years previously. His description of what he saw gives a clue to what things must have been like here in 1607:

> On my arrival at Chepstow, I walked to the bridge. It was low water and I looked down on the river ebbing between forty and fifty feet beneath; six hours after it rose nearly 40 feet, almost reaching the floor of the bridge, and flowed up with great rapidity. The channel in this place being narrow in proportion to the Severn and confined between perpendicular cliffs, the great rise and fall of the river are particularly manifest; hence it has been echoed from one publication to another that the tide at Chepstow is higher than in any other place in the world, at an average of 50-60 feet and on some extraordinary occasions not less than seventy feet.

To ascertain the truth of this assertion I plumbed the river, with the assistance of Mr Jennings and an experienced boatman, at high tide on 4th September. The perpendicular height from the bottom of the channel to the surface of the water was 47 feet 3 inches; from the water to the floor of the bridge, six feet and 2 feet 10 inches to a notch in the rail which marks the greatest rise.

Coxe was perhaps less impressed than he should have been, commenting: 'Hence the highest tide during the memory of the present generation does not exceed 56 feet 1 inch which, though very considerable, is by no means greater than that of many other places on the globe'.

I fear that the Archdeacon was mistaken. Geographers now agree that the tidal range in the Severn Estuary is second only to the Bay of Fundy in Newfoundland. However, he adds:

The rapidity of the flood up the Severn and Wye is more remarkable than its height. The cause of this rapid rise at Chepstow is derived from the projection of the rocks at Beachley and Aust, just above the mouth of the Wye, which turn part of the tide with great violence into the river.

Mud exposed at low tide River Wye, Chepstow.

Just imagine the consequences of a tsunami or storm surge coming up from the estuary and added to the highest tides!

Lydney

The villages between the Severn Estuary and the Forest of Dean, such as Alvington and Aylburton, are on higher ground along what is now the A48 and would have been out of danger in 1607 although their low-lying pastureland may have been affected.

Lydney Pill had been used as a port since Roman times and until the seventeenth-century ships could reach the town. However, the Severn then changed its course, possibly as a result of changes caused by the disaster of 1607, and the town was cut off. It was not until the development of tramways bringing minerals from the Forest of Dean that it became significant. A canal and the harbour which still exists were constructed enabling the export of coal and timber. Trade declined throughout the nineteenth century, corresponding with the rise in importance of the docks at Sharpness.

The Severn seems to have changed its course here – and at nearby Awre. Samuel Rudder in his *New History of Gloucestershire* (1779) wrote that:

> The New Grounds here are a tract of a thousand acres of land next to the river … I cannot learn for a certainty when the waters first deserted these grounds … [and] the Severn abate of its former height and power and confine itself within a narrower channel so as to leave dry this tract of land which it once overflowed, an operation not to be accounted for by all our philosophy.
>
> Whatever the cause, I am inclined to think it was not sudden but gradual and progressive and that even the old meadows here, which lie higher and further up, are acquisitions from the river, though of longer standing.
>
> I am inclined to think so from a tradition, which the inhabitants still have among them, that the tide in its usual course formerly came up to a bank of earth called The Turret, just without the churchyard, and that a large ship was built near the place where there is now a spring of fine water, called the Turret Well.
>
> These are changes in the terraqueous globe brought about in a long course of time which, however, happens seldomer in this country than in most others.

Rudder's jingoistic complacency that dramatic changes in the 'terraqueous globe' rarely happen in Britain would not have been much comfort to those unfortunate souls living further downstream in 1607.

Awre

Much of the parish of Awre is composed of land reclaimed from the Severn. The main channel may even have shifted significantly over time. Sometime before 1234, land claimed by Awre was awarded to Slimbridge which lies on the opposite bank. Land to the east of the church slopes down to lowland drained by a network of reens which was once open fields. An old sea wall which once marked the boundary of this area survived until the early twentieth century. Such areas would have been very vulnerable in 1607 and further land was lost to erosion until new defences were built in the nineteenth century.

Newnham on Severn

Newnham's position on a hill overlooking the Severn can be seen very clearly from the railway between Lydney and Gloucester. It is possible that the land was first settled on here because it was conceivable to cross the river on foot at this section when both the tide and river flow were low – although definitely not without expert local knowledge! Samuel Rudder in his 1779 history of the county states: 'Here is a ford over which, at low water, wagons and people on horseback, of more resolution than prudence, sometimes pass. Many have lost their lives in the attempt.' One who failed to heed the warning – and who should have known better – was the Vicar of Arlingham, Revd J.L. Crawley, who was drowned when he rashly attempted to cross on horseback on 29 August 1848.

A ferry between Newnham and Arlingham existed from the thirteenth century but is believed to have operated from a point about half a mile south of Newnham at Portland Nab. This site appears to have been abandoned early in the seventeenth century, again possibly as a result of the events of 1607. In 1792, the *British Universal Directory* entry for Newnham stated that 'here is a very safe ferry over the Severn which is near a mile wide'. The cliff here is constantly threatened by erosion. Margaret Willis, in *The Ferry between Newnham and Arlingham* (1993), writes that a waterman named Alfred Knight recalled from a century before that 'a hundred people could have danced on the Nab'.

Willis also records that in 1813 one William Fuller came to Newnham and afterwards wrote of 'tidal waves rising mountainous high' and 'turbulent flooding which runs with uncommon violence for miles, inundating the lowlands to a vast extent, foaming and raging like a hideous whirlpool'. He was probably thinking of the Severn Bore, for which Newnham and Arlingham are popular viewpoints, but his words could equally well be a description of the Great Flood.

Newnham seen from across the Severn at Arlingham.

St Peter's Church stands on the highest point, overlooking the Severn. The first church on the site was built in 1380, replacing an earlier church on a lower site that was damaged by floods. It was rebuilt in 1874 and again, after a fire, in 1881. It is worth visiting for the grand view across to Arlingham on the opposite bank, and beyond to Gloucester. In 1607 much of this vista would have been affected by flooding.

Over Bridge

Over Bridge was, for many centuries, the main approach to Gloucester from Wales and the Forest of Dean. The Domesday Book referred to a bridge in the area in 1086. In the mid-sixteenth century the historian and traveller John Leland described a bridge of eight arches of moderate span 'not yet finished' connected by 'a great causeway with divers double-arched bridges to drain the meadow at floods'. These arches were a hindrance to navigation, and in 1818 they were damaged by ice being carried down the river.

A new bridge, designed by Thomas Telford, was opened in 1831 and still exists 100 yards downstream from the modern structure that replaced it in 1974.

GLOUCESTER TO BRISTOL

One of the most important historical sources for Gloucestershire, already quoted with regard to Lydney, is Samuel Rudder, whose *A New History of Gloucestershire* was published in 1779. Not a leisured antiquarian like Archdeacon Coxe, mingling with the great and the good, Rudder was an artisan, the son of a pig-killer (whose gravestone states he was a lifelong vegetarian) from Uley near Stroud. Samuel moved from there and set up in business as a printer and bookseller in Cirencester.

He conceived the notion of revising and correcting what he saw as errors in Sir Robert Atkyn's magisterial *Ancient and Present State of Gloucestershire*, which was published in 1712. As Nicholas M. Henderson describes in his introduction to a new edition of Rudder's book in 2006, 'Atkyn's book had become the accepted wisdom on the county's history and there were some who regarded as presumptuous Rudder's attempt to replace it. As further grounds for their prejudice, this latest venture into a field of study that cultivated gentlemen and learned clerics had annexed as their own was made by a tradesman of modest standing and humble origins.'

Rudder was nothing if not conscientious. Over a period of twelve years he visited every parish in the county, studying the parish registers and interrogating inhabitants. He sent questionnaires to leading landowners and presented his wealth of detail in alphabetical order of parishes, following a very full account of the city of Gloucester itself.

Like all writers, he had his hobby-horses. One of these was the health of the local populations. He was convinced that the low-lying areas alongside the Severn were unhealthy in the extreme, comparing their 'impure and unwholesome air' with the Cotswolds where, he claimed 'a Cirencester doctor declared that nobody in his profession could earn a living'. His entry for Thornbury is typical:

A great part of the parish, next to the Severn is very subject to inundations from the river. Near two thousand acres of land are rated for the repairs of the sea walls ... [and] liable to floods, where the waters stagnate on the marshes and low levels. Hence the inhabitants of that part of the parish are very unhealthy from the putrid air they breathe. If any go from the hill country to reside there, such persons are usually attacked with a virulent ague on their first settling which emaciates them and proves fatal in a little time.

Even in Thornbury itself, some distance from the Severn shore 'the air is in some degree contaminated by the stagnant waters of the lowlands', and in nearby Oldbury on Severn the unhealthiness is made more so by 'the great numbers of elm trees, standing so thick about the houses, that the air has not a free current'.

We shall come across Rudder's prejudice against the lowlands again at Arlingham but it is only right to point out that he was open-minded enough to quote the comments of a Dr Frankland that 'the gentry of England are remarkably afraid of moisture and of air but seamen, who live perpetually in moist air, are always healthy if they have good provisions.'

Gloucester

Gloucester's site, on the edge of the flat and low-lying flood plain to the east of the Severn means that the city has always been vulnerable to flooding. The course of the river has shifted over time and at Gloucester is split between a western and an eastern branch. The eastern arm once had another subdivision, known latterly as Old Severn, which gradually silted up.

Gloucester's original quay was on Old Severn but by the thirteenth century its silting resulted in a new quay being built sometime before 1390 on the surviving eastern branch of the river, just to the west of the City Centre, flanked on one side by Alney Island and what is now the Ring Road. It gained in importance after 1580 when Queen Elizabeth I granted Gloucester port status, allowing it to trade with cities abroad.

As ships increased in size, Gloucester's position became increasingly unsuitable, with cargo having to be transhipped at Bristol. This led ultimately to the building of the Gloucester and Sharpness Canal and Gloucester Docks.

Most accounts of the 1607 flood refer to areas 'up as far as Gloucester' being affected but do not refer to damage in the city itself. However, in an online discussion on the effects of the flood (www.rootschat.com), a contributor styling himself as 'Bristolloggerheads' comments: 'Records around this time are particularly absent. For instance,

'West Prospect of Gloucester' by Johannes Kip. (*c.* 1725)

if trying to ascertain the impact on coastal trade by looking at the Gloucester Port Books, you will find nothing from 1606 until 1612'.

If you mention flooding to Gloucester folk, people will recall the disastrous events of 2007 or 1947 – years ending in 7 seem to be particularly inauspicious for the city – which live on in the memory. There were other bad floods in 1770 and 1795 which are fully described in Chris Witts' 2002 book *Disasters on the Severn*.

But for accounts of 1607 we must move on downstream.

Arlingham

In *The Buildings of England: Gloucestershire and the Forest of Dean* (2002) David Verey and Alan Brooks describe Arlingham as 'situated in a remote loop of the Severn, where the river travels nearly eight miles to progress little more than one, and even more isolated since the closure of the ferry to Newnham'.

One of the fullest and most dramatic descriptions of the Great Flood is found in Arlingham's parish registers. An entry for '20th January 1606-7' states that:

> There was in Arlingham ... an exceeding great flood, and the greater by reason of the south-west wind, so high that one might have moored a boat at Thomas Vinge's gate, when many lost their sheep and other cattle and their goods. Horsecroft and Newbridge being then sown with wheat and all overflowed ... Many, about the number of twenty, had lost their lives or, at the least, been greatly endangered to be starved to death. Mr Thomas Yate and his eldest son, Mr Richard Yate, were then hemmed in upon the Glass Cliff with the water ... It exceeded the flood that was about 46 years before, a foot and a half at the least than it was then.

The entry concludes with an ominous injunction: 'Cursed be the hand that raseth [erases] this memorable Record out of this Book'.

Finally there is a story that brings home the effect of this unexpected trauma on the lives of ordinary people: 'Upon this same day Mrs Anne (who was then not churched) for fear of the waters was, with Mr Childe the Vicar and his family, fain to be hurried over with the boat from the Vicarage'. (Churching, it should perhaps be explained, was a purification ritual that devout women were expected to undergo as soon as possible after giving birth.)

Arlingham Church.

It is no wonder, given its location on a flat peninsula almost entirely enclosed by a meander of the Severn, that Arlingham should have suffered greatly in 1607. The village is well worth visiting for its fourteenth-century church and evocative rural location. The church was locked when we visited late one afternoon in March 2013, so it was not possible to see the fourteenth-century stained glass for which it is famed, though the graveyard boasted many finely carved headstones. A slight mystery was the Welsh flag flying from the tower though St David's Day had already passed. Do they know something we don't or was it something to do with the rugby?

Opposite the church were the remains of the boundary wall of Arlingham Court, the home of the Yate family and dating from about 1500. Beyond the village a lane leads for about a mile to the far end of the meander bend of the Severn. From outside the Old Passage Inn there is a view across the river to Newnham Church, high on the river cliff.

Samuel Rudder was not impressed with the efficacy of these ditches, writing:

The air is made very unwholesome by the copious humid exhalations from the river and from the lands that are so frequently overflowed. This occasions inveterate agues and all those disorders incident to a low damp situation in which the poorer sort of people have manifestly the disadvantage in point of health.

Slimbridge

Slimbridge is best known today for the extensive wetlands reserve on the banks of the Severn, an area which shows how much of the levels on either side of the estuary would have looked in 1607. In *Gloucestershire Notes & Queries* William Frith, the churchwarden, gives a vivid description of the impact of the storm in 1703:

> The dreadful storm did this church little damage, but the tide drowned the greatest part of the sheep on our common, as it likewise did, besides many cows, between this place and Bristol and on the opposite shore. In the midst of this churchyard grew a vast tree, thought to be the most large and nourishing elm in the land, which was torn up by the roots ... The trunk together with the roots is well judged to be thirteen ton at least and the limbs to make six loads of billets with faggots. About two years since our minister observed that the circumambient boughs dropped round above two hundred yards. He has given it for a singers' seat in our church with this inscription thereon: 'Nov 27 A.D. 1703. Miserere'.

The nature reserve is on an area of land close to the Severn and known as the New Grounds. Samuel Rudder writes:

> [it] consists of above a thousand acres which have been gained from the Severn many years ago and belonging to the Earl of Berkeley because his manors extend to the middle of the river. Charles I commenced a suit in the Exchequer against Lord Berkeley for these lands but, after the jury was empanelled and the evidence begun, the Attorney General dropped the suit.
>
> I could never learn when this acquisition was first made from the river and perhaps it is not recorded. The like happened at Lydney.
>
> Against one side of the New Grounds, next to the river, the Earl of Berkeley (I believe the grandfather of the present earl) built a vast wall of large stones, firmly cramped together to break the violence of the waves and to preserve the land from being washed away by floods and high tides. This work is called the Hock Crib.

New Grounds, Slimbridge.

Was this work, three generations before 1779, a belated response to damage done by the 1607 flood? We may never know.

Rudder also tells us that the New Grounds were valuable grazing land because 'it is thought the herbage has stronger nutritive powers and makes the cattle fat sooner than the grass of the common meadows'. The area was also used for growing samphire, 'which is much esteemed in pickling and sometimes used in medicine'.

Berkeley

Berkeley, on its low sandstone ridge, overlooks Berkeley Pill. Once the site of a Saxon minster, in 1607 it was still a significant port and local trading centre, the Pill providing what was described a few years later as 'a pretty safe haven'. In 1540, Leland wrote, 'The town of Berkeley is no great thing but it standeth well and in very good soil.'

Like other places along the estuary it was protected by a sea wall. In 1703, the method of construction of this wall was described by Revd Henry Head in an account of the Great Storm, and it would have been much the same a century before:

Made of great stones and sticks, which they call rouses, a yard and a half long, about the bigness of one's thigh, rammed into the ground as firm as possible in many places and levelled it almost to the ground, forcing vast quantities of earth a great distance from the shore, and stones, many of which were above a hundredweight.

There are no contemporary accounts of what happened here in 1607 but the place certainly suffered in 1703. In a contribution to *Gloucestershire Notes & Queries*, Head described how:

the River Severn beat down and tore to pieces the sea wall and was let in above a mile over part of the parish and did great damage to the land. It carried away one house which was by the sea side and a gentleman's stable, wherein was a horse, into the next ground, and the stable fell to pieces and so the horse came out.

The church did not escape damage either. Mr Head, in some awe, wrote:

Twenty-six sheets of lead, hanging all together, were blown off from the middle aisle of our church, which is a large one, without touching it, and into the churchyard ten yards distance from the church and were took up all joined together as they were on the roof. The plumber told me that the sheets weighed each three hundred[weight] and a half.

The metal thieves, who have become such a plague to churches in modern times, would have been envious that the difficult part of the job had, apparently, been done for them by the hand of God!

Aust
The pamphlet *God's Warning to his people of England* makes it clear that the effects of the disaster were long-lasting, saying of Aust that:

Many passengers that are ferried over there now are fain to be guided by guides all along the Causies [causeways], where the water still remaineth for the space of three or four miles, or else they will be in great danger of drowning, the water lieth as yet so deep there. Many dead carcasses, both there and in many other places are daily found floating upon the waters and as yet cannot be known who they are or what number of persons are drowned.

The first Seven Bridge stretches dramatically across the river between here and Beachley, but before the bridge was opened in 1966, motorists endured lengthy delays on the ferry slipway. Crossing here was never easy and would have been very dangerous back in the seventeenth century and before. Samuel Rudder described the restrictions in 1779, demonstrating how the elements had to be respected, even in normal conditions:

> It is of great importance to travellers to know the time of passing [i.e when it is possible to cross] ... The passage here depends on the wind and the tide. The southerly, westerly and northerly winds are proper for passing but when wind and tide go the same way, there is no passing; therefore, when the wind is northerly it must be at flood, or coming in of the tide, and then you may pass for five hours. On the contrary, when the wind is southerly or westerly, all passing must be at ebb or going out of the tide, which affords seven hours good passing.

Old Passage House, down on the shoreline, dates from the eighteenth century but has sixteenth-century origins. It marks the point where passengers would have boarded the little ferry boat in those days – possibly after saying their prayers! And with good cause. On 1 September 1839 the ferryboat *Dispatch* went down halfway across. The master, Captain Whitchurch, who knew the river, had been reluctant because of the conditions and was persuaded 'against his better judgement' to risk it. He drowned, along with his son and about ten others, including a young boy. A dog escaped by swimming ashore. Four years later, Captain Whitchurch's other son was among all hands lost when another ferry sank.

The village of Aust is half a mile away 'behind a sheltering hill' as Lewis Wilshire described it in *Berkeley Vale and Severn Shore* (1954). 'It is a small place now,' he wrote, 'just a group of cottages, a church and a few scattered farms'. He called at the Boar's Head Inn, which still survives to this day, but without its sign that once warned motorists that it was 'positively the last tavern this side of the ferry'.

Rockhampton

The fourteenth-century tower and fifteenth-century south door of St Oswald's Church in Rockhampton would have existed in 1607. It is a scattered village strung out along a lane north of Thornbury. Rudder wrote: 'The soil is rich and mostly in pasturage but the parts next to the Severn are subject to inundations which sometimes do considerable damage.' The parish register records that in 1606 (old style) 'The sea did overflow the banks and sea-walls insomuch that very many people and cattle were drowned all along Severne side between Bristowe and Gloucester'.

Olveston

There is something of a mystery surrounding Olveston. Verey and Brookes state that the church has a tower with an 'embattled parapet and overlarge pinnacles of 1606, rebuilt after the former spire had been struck by lightning'. Allowing for the previously mentioned calendar confusion, was this the occasion of the Great Flood and evidence of the disaster being caused by a storm surge rather than a tsunami? Yet some contemporary accounts refer to it being a fine and sunny morning.

Lewis Wilshire, in *Berkeley Vale and Severn Shore* (1954, reprinted 1980), refers to an account of the storm written by 'an Olveston schoolmaster' which is in the Bodleian Library at Oxford. He gives the title as *Fearful Newes of Thunder and Lightning, with terrible effects thereof, which Almightie God sent on a place called Olverstone in the County of Gloucester the 26th of November last … having prefixed before it, a short discourse concerning two other admirable accidents that soon after ensued. Truly related by P.S. and dedicated to the King's most excellent Maiestie. Printed by G. Eld for Francis Burton, 1606.*

This only serves to add to the confusion. The date 1606 seems clear enough but 26 November was the day of the 1703 storm, not the 1606/7 flood.

Whichever year the storm struck Olveston, it seems to have been apocalyptic:

The morning of the day being lowering and sad did yet, a little after eight, begin to smile … Before nine there came up a strong wind from the west, bringing up a most dark mantle that overspread the whole heavens. Thereafter appeared a rainbow which in turn was followed by a great darkness and a frightful hailstorm which left the ground more than six inches deep in hailstones. Then did the wind make a terrible rattle and there were fearful flashes of lightning and soon there were three or four claps of thunder, louder than ordinary. Whereof I took occasion to talk to the gentlewoman of the house … to this effect, that the atheists of the world as did not know, acknowledge and fear God had great cause to be terrified … but such as did truly fear God, they need not be appalled or dismayed.

It seems that the worthy schoolmaster was so pleased with his little sermon that he was soon repeating it to his pupils in the schoolhouse. He was interrupted by the urgent clanging of the church bells. He sent a boy out to find out the cause of the disturbance and soon received the awful news that the church had been struck and the steeple was on fire!

But when did this happen? 1607 or 1703? I fear that I have been totally flummoxed by this game of Chinese Whispers among historians. It sounds more like 1703 to me but why then are we told that the tower was rebuilt in 1606?

Opposite the church there is a cottage which has a massive window lintel downstairs, with a housing for a halved joint of a type that would have been used in the former spire. The cottage is built filling the gap between two older ones but unfortunately there is nothing in the present structure to precisely date its construction.

Almondsbury

One of the most important primary sources for the Great Flood is an account written by the Vicar of Almondsbury, Revd John Paul, and dated by him in the old style, 20 January 1606. He describes:

> The River Severn rose upon a sodden Tuesday morning, the 20th January, being ... the highest tide after the change of the moon ... by reason of a mighty strong western wind. So that from Minehead to Slimbridge the low grounds along the river were that turning tide overflowed. In Saltmarsh many houses were overthrown, sundry Christians drowned, hundreds of cattle and horses perished and thousands of sheep and lambs were lost. Unspeakable were the spoil and losses on both sides of the river. The salt water was in Rednyng [Redwick near Pilning] in Sansom's new chamber to the upper step save two and in Hobbe's house six foot high. In Ellenhurst, at Wade's house, the sea rose near seven feet and in some houses there it ran in at one window and out at another. In Bristol, by credible report, the morning tide was higher than that at evening tide by nine foot of water.

Rudder wrote of Almondsbury that 'there is more pasture than arable land and a great deal of marshy land towards the Severn. 1,342 acres are particularly liable to be overflowed by the river'.

Almondsbury Church.

Pilning

'Ellenhurst' in the Vicar's account has been identified by architectural historian Linda J. Hall as Little Ellinghurst Farm, formerly in Pilning parish but since demolished. In her report on the building she noted: 'The tremendously thick walls of the kitchen end (well over three feet thick) suggest a medieval origin.' She considered that the house would have once had an open hall, and the parlour had sixteenth-century moulded beams. The house's long, low profile was typical of a former longhouse with rooms for the family on one side of the central passage and a cow byre on the other.

As such, Little Ellinghurst was a rare example of a pre-1607 house that somehow survived the flood. As on the Gwent Levels across the river, older houses are very hard to find. Another still surviving is Ostbridge Manor Farm in Olveston parish, an attractive stone building on the lane from Tockington towards Pilning station. On the front of the house is a projection which once housed the garderobe (medieval privy) while inside the house are original doorframes and a roof structure which includes magnificent windbraces.

Ostbridge Manor Farm.

Redwick (Gloucestershire)

The road through Pilning leads on to Redwick and New Passage. Before
the Severn Tunnel was opened in 1886, rail passengers for South Wales
had to board a ferry to Portskewett here. This Redwick should not be
confused with the Redwick on the Gwent Levels, though the derivation of
the name is the same. The two Redwicks are only about eight miles apart
across the estuary, though not directly opposite each other, unlike the two
Purtons near Sharpness and Lydney respectively. From New Passage there
are bracing walks along the sea wall in either direction, with views of the
two Severn Bridges and across to Wales and the Forest of Dean. On the
landward sides are the flat landscapes that would have been defenceless
once the primitive sea defences were breached in 1607.

Lewis Wilshire's *Berkeley Vale and Severn Shore* (1954) quotes a letter
received by His Majesty's Commissioners of Sewers. This describes how
'the Great Flood came down into John Hortt's orchard in Redwick'.
The sea wall was breached 'and never since made up sufficiently to defend
the same. At every high tide we, your poor suppliants, being dwellers
there, be greatly dammified and almost undone thereby'. It seems the
necessary repairs were then carried out at a cost of £4.

Hallen

For *Berkeley Vale and Severn Shore*, Wilshire interviewed Clem Hignell of Norton Farm near Henbury. He remembered when 'sixty-eight years ago [the late 1880s] the Severn came inland as far as Hallen – only for a few hours but the salt water got into the wells and spoiled the water. Many cows and pigs were drowned.' Mr Hignell also remembered 'some forty years ago, when Severn Beach was isolated for three weeks'.

BRISTOL

Bristol's location, several miles from the Severn along the Avon Gorge, might seem to have offered some protection from the raging waters but John Latimer's *Annals of Bristol: Sixteenth and Seventeenth Centuries*, published in 1900–8 (new edition by Kingsmead Reprints in 1970), describes how:

> A phenomenal flood tide occurred in the Severn on the morning of January 20th 1607 whereby the low-lying lands on each bank of the river from Gloucester downwards were inundated over some hundreds of square miles. The loss of life was estimated at five hundred and a greater number of people were saved only by climbing upon trees, haystacks and roofs of houses. In Bristol the tide, being partially dammed back by the bridge flowed over Redcliff, St Thomas and Temple Streets to a depth of several feet. St Stephen's Church and the quays were deeply flooded and the loss of goods in cellars and warehouses was enormous.

'Now bend your eyes upon the city of Bristowe,' wrote one contemporary chronicler, 'and there behold as much cause of lamentation as in any place of this realm.'

Exploring these streets today, the visitor will not find much that would have been there in 1607. Aside from the tower, St Thomas's was rebuilt in 1789-93 but St Stephen's, with its majestic Somerset-style tower, remains substantially the same, though restored in 1875-98. The streets still follow their old alignment and alongside Bristol Bridge it can be seen how it could have acted as a dam, blocking the wave of water as it rushed up the Frome, causing it to flood the streets on either side.

In 1607, of course, the River Frome had not been covered over by the roads now known as Colston Avenue in Bristol's Centre. St Stephen's,

St Stephen's Church and River Frome, Bristol.

whose tower can still be seen beyond more recent buildings, was close to a bustling quayside with ships moored right in the heart of the city. In 1739 Alexander Pope described how 'in the middle of the street, as far as you can see, hundreds of ships, their masts as thick as they can stand one by another'. The river was culverted in 1892 to become what was for many years known as The Tramways Centre and is still the city's transport hub.

The centre of the old city continued to suffer from flooding after 1607. One of the worst occasions was in 1738 when Latimer records that 'a prodigious flood occurred in the Avon and Frome on 10th January, owing to protracted rains'. Many of the same streets were submerged, and goods stored in cellars and warehouses near the quay were destroyed at considerable financial cost to their owners. The following year, according to Latimer, two houses in Bridge Street were undermined by the water and collapsed. He also refers to bad floods in 1875, 1882 and 1896 when, following heavy rain, the floodwaters flowed over the top of the outer lock-gates at Cumberland Basin and houses were inundated at St Philip's Marsh, Bedminster and down river at Pill.

Today it is estimated that 30,000 houses in Bristol are at risk of flooding, either from a massive tidal surge as in 1607, the rivers bursting their banks or the run-off from nearby hills after heavy rain. In November 2012 one of the first acts of Bristol's newly elected mayor, George Ferguson, was to speak out in favour of a £50 million tidal barrier on the Avon to protect the city from flooding for 'decades to come', but he opposed a Severn Barrage as this would damage the prospects of the Port of Bristol.

Plans for such a barrier first emerged in the run-up to the mayoral election, but Liberal Democrat Councillor Tim Kent told the media that experts had been looking at the idea for some time. The initial idea had been to build it near the Clifton Suspension Bridge but it was now considered that it would be more effective if it was built at Avonmouth, although no specific site had been identified. Anything that affected the iconic view of the Suspension Bridge would, of course, have met fierce resistance.

Mr Kent added that such a barrier would be unlikely to be built for another ten or fifteen years, but that they had to think ahead because of rising sea levels and also the massive costs involved. He pointed out that the times when the city is most prone to flooding were during spring tides when the Avon reaches its highest level and water often spills out onto the A4 Portway. For years, he said, it had been assumed that the docks could absorb any excess water but engineers had warned that in such an emergency they could only do so for about thirty minutes before levels became too high. Areas of the city close to the Frome and Brislington Brook, Whitchurch, Withywood, Hartcliffe and Avonmouth were all at risk, as well as the city centre and the new Enterprise Zone near Temple Meads.

Its supporters would argue that the Severn Barrage between Cardiff and Weston-super-Mare would offer the necessary flood protection as well as generating much-needed electricity. The new mayor was, however, not in favour. 'The financial and environmental risks are too great,' George Ferguson said, referring to the potential loss of investment and jobs in the Port of Bristol if the barrage was built.

SOMERSET

Kingston Seymour

'The sea has several times tried to swallow this rich marshland village,' wrote Arthur Mee in *The King's England: Somerset*. 'Painted on wood in the church is an old account of the time when the waves broke down the village defences and filled the Norman font with sea water. For ten days the flood was five feet deep, the water above the pews.'

Hanging in the church porch, this memorial to the 1607 flood reads thus:

January 20 1606 & 4th of Jas I. An inundation of the sea water by overflowing and breaking down of the sea banks; happened in this Parish of Kingstone-Seamore, and many others adjoining; by reason whereof many Persons were drown'd and much Cattle and Goods were lost: the water in the Church was five feet high and the greatest part lay on the ground about ten days. William Bower.

After the flooding, the fields were found to be too wet and boggy for cattle for many years and the prevailing dampness was said to cause ague in local people.

Surrounded on all sides by deep and steep-sided rhines, the church stands in the centre of the village on what is effectively a moated site. An ancient lychgate, with a well-worn plank on which to base a coffin,

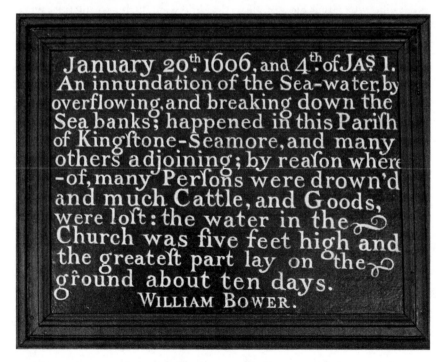

The flood board, Kingston Seymour Church.

stands at the meeting of green lanes. Unfortunately, the church was locked when we visited but the recently restored board commemorating the flood can be seen in the porch. East of the church is a weather-worn tomb chest that pre-dates the flood. As you stand among the graves, the roar from the motorway, just a couple of fields away, could be mistaken for the sound of an approaching tidal wave.

Despite its nearness to the M5, Kingston Seymour still seems very remote. In daylight you still need a good map to navigate your way past houses now some distance from the sea but still bearing such significant names as Wharf Farm, Channel View and Seawall Farm. Tutshill Farm and Dowlais Farm intriguingly hint at links with places on the opposite side of the Bristol Channel. Mariners from North Somerset and Devon would have been familiar with the waters and harbours of the estuary in the days when it was a highway rather than a barrier.

Wick St Lawrence

More from Arthur Mee's *The King's England: Somerset* book of 1941:

> The dykes do their best to cut it off from its neighbours … A stone tells in rhyme the sad story of a man and his horse who, 300 years ago, were caught fast in the mire where the Yeo empties into the sea and were held fast there till the sea came in and drowned them.

Muriel Searle, in *Somerset – Green and Pleasant Land* (1975), also has this story and describes Wick St Lawrence as 'remote and unspoiled. Here we come back to the Somerset moors again, to the country of dykes and pastures. The village is noted for its cider-apple orchards but ironically it has no public house. Like much of low-lying Somerset, this area was once under water or mire.'

Brean and Berrow

In 1607, according to the contemporary accounts, Brean was 'swallowed up' – seven of its nine houses were destroyed and twenty-six inhabitants drowned. It was reported that John Good of Brean lost his wife and nine servants when the wave struck, but saved himself by clinging onto a chunk of thatch that carried him for more than a mile before being washing him up on dry land. Thatch also saved the wife and son of John Stow of Berrow but Stow himself and three other children drowned.

Brean and Berrow lie in a vulnerable location where the Somerset Levels reach the coast and have always been at risk of inundation. The extensive area of beach and sand dunes along this stretch makes it popular with visitors and there are many caravan and camp sites. These can only be reached by a narrow access road from the direction of Burnham on Sea which can get very congested at the height of the summer season. The Somerset Coastal Change Pathfinder Project, a joint initiative by DEFRA and the County Council (www.somersetcoastalchange.org.uk), has expressed concern about what would happen if there was a sudden flood here. 'It would be of great benefit', says its website, 'if this risk could be acknowledged and visitors informed of what procedures to follow if the worst scenario were to occur.'

According to the website, the Pathfinder Project is concerned that 'currently there is no official and consistent management plan for the dunes and beach because responsibility for their maintenance is undertaken voluntarily by three groups, Brean Parish Council, Sedgemoor District Council and the Berrow Conservation Group. Each group has a slightly different management approach' – but the project admits that 'each has done an admirable job of monitoring the beach and dunes.'

The River Axe flows between Uphill Cliff and Brean Down before reaching the sea. The flat landscape and high tidal range pose an inevitable flood risk, so high that levees have been built along its banks and sluice gates at Bleadon to minimise the flood risk. However, there are worries about whether this would be sufficient to cope with a storm surge approaching from the north west. A particular concern is the risk of 'back-door flooding', where the flood waters would encroach from behind the defences as opposed to overtopping them. This was the cause of much of the flood damage near Gloucester in 2007.

In 2011 this part of Somerset was the location for a controversial proposal by the Environment Agency to abandon hundreds of acres of land to the sea. The agency wanted to move the flood defences between Clevedon and Kewstoke up to a mile further inland in order to create an area of mudflat and salt marsh habitat to meet European Union laws that required the creation of new intertidal habitat to compensate for land lost to sea level rise or other uses elsewhere in the estuary. The first phase would see 195 acres of salt marsh recreated by 2030 and a further 702 by 2060. It was estimated that at Kingston Seymour about 22 per cent of the parish would cease to be farmland and become flooded, at least intermittently.

Notwithstanding the fact that the Environment Agency's claim that the scheme would protect about 37,000 people from the risk of flooding, the plan was massively controversial. More than a hundred residents of Kingston Seymour attended a meeting to voice their concerns to North Somerset MP, Dr Liam Fox. The National Farmers' Union and the North Somerset Flood Risk Action Group (NSFRAG) also lobbied against the proposals. 'At a time of mounting concern about food security why sacrifice highly productive agricultural land?' North Somerset NFU Secretary Mike Clements asked. The Environment Agency replied that farmers affected would be offered grants under a Country Stewardship Scheme to help them change their way of farming.

Later in the year, following pressure from Dr Fox and fellow Somerset MPs John Penrose and Ian Liddell-Granger, Government minister Richard Benyon instructed the Environment Agency to review its plans. Agency spokesman Paul Gainey told the media that the Agency was taking 'time out' to do as requested. NSFRAG secretary Leonie Allday said, 'We are pleased to know that this re-think will take place. This scheme is not going to go away but we are hoping that any future schemes will be more reasonable and take more account of the needs of local people and communities.'

Berrow Church stands amid the dunes half a mile from the sea. It would have been surrounded by the floodwaters in 1607. When we visited, the main door (dated 1707) was blocked by a metal floodgate but the small priest's door in the chancel wall had a 'welcome' sign on it. Inside there are many architectural features that survive from before the flood, as well as a beam from the former West Gallery which bears an inscription of 1637. It is worthwhile, after visiting the church, to climb up from the churchyard into the dunes to admire the extensive views along the coast.

Northwards from Berrow, the large houses and smaller bungalows give way to a temporary looking landscape of holiday chalets, amusement parks, caravans and fish and chip shops. A track leads down to Brean Sands where cars can be parked right on the beach. In February 2013 a picture of this bleak and windswept location appeared in the free newspaper *Metro* under the startling headline: 'Under this patch of sand is the secret of U.S. Security.' According to reporter James Day, it is somewhere along this stretch of coast that the 13,000 kilometre undersea fibre optic cable carrying the vital internet links between America and Britain come ashore. 'One snip could lead to a digital blackout', Mr Day wrote. He was taken to a communications centre 'flanked by frozen-food factories on an

Brean Sands.

industrial estate in Somerset' but was 'forbidden from revealing its exact address'. Apparently it was one of a number of sites declared a 'critical foreign dependency' by the U.S. Department of Homeland Security – and then revealed in the Wikileaks scandal of 2012. Assuming (as seems likely) that this secret facility is somewhere nearby on the Somerset Levels, I hope it has adequate flood defences!

There is still a survivor of pre-1607 Brean. Looking slightly forlorn alongside the busy road through the holiday parks is St Bridget's Church whose tower has a distinctive saddleback roof. The church was first built in the thirteenth century but is much restored. The pulpit dates from 1620 – was this a somewhat delayed replacement for an earlier one wrecked in the flood? We shall probably never know.

Burnham on Sea

The need for good sea defences in North Somerset was dramatically demonstrated on the night of 13 December 1981, when storm-force winds in the Bristol Channel combined with high tides to cause widespread flooding. The tidal surge flooded more than 12,500 acres, even reaching the M5. Over a thousand homes and businesses were affected. Miraculously there were no human casualties but thousands of acres of farmland between Clevedon and Porlock were inundated and damage was estimated at over £6 million.

Burnham was the worst affected. The sea wall collapsed in several places, leaving gaping holes in pavements and road surfaces. A car parked on the seafront was hurled against a house, damaging its walls and windows. Around 400 properties were flooded. The local authority arranged for stone from local quarries to be brought in by lorries to be used in emergency repairs, and volunteers on the beach filled sandbags.

Since 1981 the Environment Agency has spent more than £60 million improving Somerset's coastal defences with major schemes at Clevedon, Weston-super-Mare, Burnham and on the River Parrett.

The figures would have been very different in 1607 but Burnham-on-Sea suffered in much the same way. Contemporary accounts tell that the sea wall at Burnham gave way and the water flowed over the low-lying levels inland as far as Glastonbury Tor, fourteen miles from the coast.

Glastonbury

Glastonbury has a mythical reputation as the Isle of Avalon, but as archaeologist Philip Rahtz explains in the *English Heritage Book of Glastonbury* (1993):

> Glastonbury is not an island and has not been one in recent geological time. It is a peninsula, linked to higher ground to the east by a neck of land nowhere lower than 33 feet above modern sea level. To travellers from the west, coming by water, it may have looked like an island, with water or watery moors on three sides as the land link was invisible from that side.

Certainly it would have seemed so in 1607 and in other times of flood when the flat fields below Glastonbury Tor were under several feet of water. Like the inhabitants of the Forest of Dean, the people of the Levels were considered 'funny folk' by those who did not live there, in-bred and with their own very curious customs unknown to outsiders. Rahtz quotes Richard Warner, writing in 1829,: 'The Levels must have been either a gloomy waste of waters, or a still more hideous expanse of reeds and other aquatic plants, impassible by human foot, and involved in an atmosphere pregnant with pestilence and death.'

The Levels' status as land rather than water is tenuous and temporary. Philip Rahtz writes:

At times the river valleys, with their changing courses would have been dry land but when the sea levels were relatively higher (the sea level rising or the land mass dropping) the whole of the lower areas could be inundated; estuarine marine sediments have been identified close to Glastonbury, dating to the first millennium BC.

He then describes how 'Glastonbury was open and exposed to the west, the flat aspect broken only by the humps of Brent Knoll and Brean Down. It could be reached from this direction by water, either directly at times of the greatest inundation, or by way of the rivers.'

Flooding may well have allowed access to Glastonbury but at other times it would have been a nightmare, not least in 1607 when floodwater extended to St John's Church with water over six-feet deep in the streets. The pastures alongside the River Brue were under up to thirteen feet of water, and hayricks floated away 'but the pigs went on eating on top … rabbits on sheep's backs were drowned with them'.

This had happened before, especially at times when the flood defences constructed in the Middle Ages by the major ecclesiastical landowners, such as Glastonbury Abbey or the Bishops of Wells, were not properly maintained. The Levels were valuable real estate. Fish and eels were raised, pigs and cattle were pastured and the waterways provided transport. However, all this depended on proper maintenance of sea walls and sluices. Rahtz shows how:

> when dykes and walls had been broken down in the early fourteenth century, it was complained that 'The water poured in and drowned 1,000 acres of corn, barley, beans, pease and oats, also 50 acres of meadowland and 300 acres of pasture … the land remained drowned for two years and things have gone from bad to worse'.

Is it possible that poorer maintenance of the dykes and defences following the Dissolution of the Monasteries in the previous century made the devastation of 1607 even worse?

Meare
In *Somersetshire: Highways, Byways and Waterways* (1894) C.R.B. Barrett gives an evocative description of the road between Glastonbury and Meare:

On either side the marshy fields are low and perfectly flat, and intersected by frequent dykes, here and there fringed with pollard willows or stunted bushes ... In the distance, amid trees as it appears, the towers of Wells Cathedral stand out white in a sudden fleeting gleam of sunshine. Beyond Wells, and forming a background, is the long range of the Mendip Hills. Not a landscape of great beauty but pleasant withal.

The church, manor house and former abbot's fish house at Meare all date from the fourteenth century, so would have been here in 1607 when the waters surged past. They would have burst open the ancient church door that is well over 600 years old now and lapped at the base of the fifteenth-century stone pulpit.

Inundation remained a problem here long after the Great Flood. The Meare Pool, finally drained in the eighteenth century, covered 500 acres every winter and there is a record in the church accounts that in 1765 the sexton was paid eighteen pence for rowing the church clock from Glastonbury.

Meare and nearby Godney are renowned for their ancient Lake Villages which date from more than 2,000 years ago. Such villages are not unique to the Somerset Levels but have been found in other similar fen landscapes in East Anglia.

Muchelney

In November 2012, the village of Muchelney (Anglo-Saxon for 'big island') provided a graphic example of the effects of flooding. It seems that the builders of the medieval church of St Peter & St Paul, immediately adjacent to the abbey, knew something that modern developers have forgotten or ignored – that building on a flood plain is a bad idea! Both these ancient buildings remained above the floodwaters that cut off the village for more than a week.

Villagers depended on 4x4s and the Burnham Area rescue boat to bring in vital supplies. The Environment Agency also brought a boat to assist in the operation. On Sunday 2 December the Revd Jess Pittman needed a lift on farmer Richard Hodder's tractor to get to the church to lead the morning service. Many of her parishioners also used tractors to get there.

Wedmore

A wall-painting in St Mary Magdalene's Church shows St Christopher carrying the young Jesus through the water, not across a river – as is more normally depicted – but apparently across the sea, as ships and a mermaid are depicted. The mermaid, however, cannot have been washed inland to Wedmore in the 1607 flood as this painting is believed to date from the late fifteenth or early sixteenth century. It is a rare and unusual survival.

Another interesting feature of the church is the memorial brass to George Hodge, dated 1630. He is dressed as a soldier of the period, complete with buff coat and breeches, boots, pike and sword. Presumably, as a Wedmore man of the early seventeenth century, he would have experienced the flood personally. What could he have told us, I wonder?

Flooding would not have been a rare event back then – and still is not now. The village stands on slightly raised ground surrounded by the flat meadows and rhines of the Somerset Levels. The River Brue regularly bursts its banks in winter and the water table remains high for much of the year. South of Wedmore are the Tealham and Tadham Moors, Sites of Special Scientific Interest, so designated because of their plants and wildlife.

The village's most unusual claim to fame (and, it has to be said, totally irrelevant to the subject of this book) is as the home of The Turnip Prize, a parody of the much more earnest Turner Prize. Started at one of the pubs in 1999 as a joke, it is an award for deliberately awful artistic non-achievement. Prompted by the exhibition of Tracey Emin's unmade bed, the basic rule is that 'you can enter anything you like but it must be rubbish'.

Tadham Moor fields in flood. (Jane Gunn, Wedmore WI)

Weston Zoyland

The dykes and ditches of the Somerset Levels played their part in English history within a lifetime of 1607. The motley band of ill-trained farm labourers, craftsmen and other men of Dorset and Somerset recruited by the Duke of Monmouth in his ill-fated rebellion against the unpopular King James II faced the Royalist troops under John Churchill, the future Duke of Marlborough, here in the Battle of Sedgemoor in 1685.

Led by Godfrey, a local herdsmen who claimed to know the area, the rebels had marched six miles from Bridgwater in the darkness over some of the most treacherous terrain in the country to confront the king's army that was camped at Weston Zoyland on the flat marshy fields of Sedgemoor.

For the 300th anniversary of the battle, the Sealed Knot staged a re-enactment and the well-known folk band Strawhead produced an LP of seventeenth-century and modern songs about Monmouth's campaign. The sleeve notes from the record take up the story:

> The moon shone full in a cloudless sky but a thick mist enveloped the moor, deadening sound. Along Bradney Lane, past Peazy Farm and over the Black Ditch, across the Longmoor Rhine – in silence and undetected they had travelled nearly three miles of the moor. They were now less than three-quarters of a mile from the Royalist camp. Still no alarm … the clock on Chedzoy steeple struck one.
>
> […]Then a single shot rang out. A trooper from the Royalist side had at last seen them through the mist and the alarm was raised. Monmouth's only chance was to attack immediately and he ordered his men on horseback to charge. At this point Godfrey was either dismissed or found himself left behind and the rebels found themselves halted by the Bussex Rhine. Their commander chose wrongly in his search for a crossing point and led his men right across the Royalist front.

The rebels never stood a chance and were helpless in the dark and in the maze of ditches. Three hundred died in the battle, a thousand more were killed in the pursuit afterwards. Many more were hunted down and tried by Judge Jeffries in the infamous Bloody Assizes that followed. Three hundred and twenty of them were hanged and hundreds more were transported into slavery.

'The Battle of Sedgemoor,' wrote Arthur Mee, 'the last battle to be fought on English soil was unutterably sad. Nothing was wanting to make the tragedy complete.'

Bridgwater

William Jones' *God's Warning to his people of England* records that:

> The country all along to Bridgwater was greatly distressed and much hurt there done. It was a pitiful sight to behold what numbers of fat oxen were there drowned, what flocks of sheep, what heads of kine have there been lost ... great reekes of fodder for cattle are floating like ships on the waters and dead beasts swimming thereon ... The tops of trees, a man may behold remaining above the waters, upon whose branches multitudes of all kind of turkeys, hens and other suchlike poultry were fain to fly up into the trees to save their lives, where many of them perished ... not being able to fly to dry land by reason of their weakness.

Bridgwater stands near the mouth of the River Parrett which, like the Severn, frequently spills over the flat meadows alongside it and which has a bore which comes upstream on occasions with the incoming tide. St Mary's Church retains fifteenth- and sixteenth-century woodwork, a finely carved pulpit, screens and other details which would have been here when the coast and countryside around were devastated by the Great Flood. The view from the fourteenth-century tower that day, when Bridgwater found itself an island in a turbulent sea, must have been apocalyptic.

West Somerset and Beyond

Steart Peninsula

West of the River Parrett, the Steart Peninsula near Bridgwater is another area where the Environment Agency is proposing that farmland is abandoned to the sea. The area has always been prone to flooding and would have been overwhelmed in 1607. It suffered in 1981 when the area around Burnham-on-Sea was badly affected.

A combination of coastal erosion, a sea level rise and wave action has led to the existing sea defences becoming vulnerable to failure, hence the proposals to move the defences back to create a more sustainable possibility of managing the flood risk. The intention is to create a new inter-tidal habitat which, as was intended around Kingston Seymour, could compensate for the loss of such areas elsewhere in the Severn Estuary. The Agency believes that this would improve the level of flood protection for local people.

Consultation on the scheme began in 2008, and two years later the Agency unveiled its plan to convert the peninsula to wetlands. They estimated that the scheme would cost between £17 and £20 million, including land purchase costs of up to £7 million. Work began on the programme in May 2012 and, when complete, it will be the largest habitat creation scheme in England.

It was a controversial decision. Ian Liddle-Granger, MP for Bridgwater and West Somerset, who had been a critic of the similar scheme proposed for the area around Kingston Seymour, condemned the project, which by now was forecast to cost £29 million, as a waste of public money. 'It is a schizophrenic scheme,' he told the *Western Daily Press*. 'It is neither a flood defence scheme nor wetland creation. It is not going to create any jobs at all.'

He said the scheme was designed to offset the possible loss of wetland in Wales to flood defences. 'That may not be needed for fifty years', he claimed. 'The Welsh are being protected to the detriment of Steart which will still face the threat of flooding.' However the Environment Agency maintained that the scheme would safeguard Steart village against flooding from the River Parrett and increase protection to the only road linking it to surrounding communities.

Combwich

Combwich (pronounced Commidge) at the landward end of the Steart Peninsula was the site of an old ferry. It was a port for the export of local produce and the import of timber from the fifteenth century. In 1723, a scheme was proposed to improve navigation on the River Parrett and shorten the journey time for boats by making an artificial cut across the base of the Steart Peninsula but after much debate locally this was not done. It seems that lack of support from landowners and concerns about the costs and financial risks involved were the main factors.

Combwich Pill had been used for seaborne trade since the fourteenth century. From the 1830s, the wharf was used by local brickworks to import coal and export tiles to Wales and Gloucestershire. This traffic ceased in the 1930s but in the late 1950s the wharf was taken over and upgraded by the Central Electricity Generating Board for the bringing in of heavy materials needed for the construction of the nuclear power stations at Hinkley Point.

Hinkley Point

Hinkley Point A power station (now closed) was begun in 1957 with a scheduled completion date of 1960 but was not in fact operational until 1965. A second power station, Hinkley Point B, was running by 1976. A third and possibly a fourth station are now planned and work has already begun by EDF Energy on Hinkley Point C.

Nuclear power stations remain controversial and Hinkley Point continues to be the scene of anti-nuclear protests. In October 2012 seven people were arrested when protestors carried out a mass trespass at the site. They intended to scatter 577 seed balls to symbolise the number of days since the Fukushima nuclear power station disaster which followed a tsunami generated by the major earthquake off the east coast of Japan the previous year. Television pictures of the tsunami shocked many and led to concerns about what would happen to the nuclear stations at Hinkley Point, Oldbury on Severn and Berkeley should there be a repeat of the 1607 event. Despite the protests, in March 2013 permission was granted for the new reactor.

A Visitor Centre at Hinkley Point gives access to a nature trail, a good opportunity for the visitor to experience the unique atmosphere on this part of the Somerset coast. Chris Willoughby wrote in the caption to his picture of Bridgwater Bay in *Photographers' Britain – Somerset* (1993) that:

> The coastline along this part of Britain is rather like the lip of a shallow bowl. The lip itself is in places only a few metres above the sea while the land behind falls away, the bottom of the bowl being several kilometres inland. It is a bay that is swept with vicious currents, and contains no sheltered inlets, picturesque fishing harbours or sophisticated holiday resorts, only miles of mud and a frothy brown sea that laps on its shore.

No wonder the whole stretch of coast from Brean Down to Hinkley Point is a cause of great concern to those whose responsibility is to guard against flooding.

Watchet

West of Hinkley Point the high ground of the Quantock Hills nears the coast and flooding becomes less of an issue, as would have been the case in 1607. There are few safe harbours along the north Somerset coast where the strong currents and high tidal range make it a dangerous area for shipping. The only commercial port is Watchet whose harbour has been active since Saxon times.

The church on the hill that overlooks Watchet is dedicated to St Decuman who is said to have arrived from Wales, drifting across on a raft accompanied by his faithful cow. It is just as well, perhaps, that this was long before 1607 or the erstwhile saint might have found himself unintentionally surfing up the estuary and all the way to Gloucester on the tidal wave. The legend says that the local inhabitants were not impressed by their new neighbour and set upon him while he was at his prayers, whereupon Decuman picked up his severed head and other possessions and set off, together with the cow, to return to Wales.

Minehead

A flat low-lying coastal strip about a mile wide lies between the Exmoor hills and Blue Anchor Bay on the approach to Minehead. This may well have suffered in 1607 and Butlins Holiday Camp at Minehead could have been under water had such a place, unimaginable then of course, existed. What could have existed in the seventeenth century was the Minehead Hobby Horse, now a familiar sight on May Day in the town and at folk music festivals in the West Country throughout the year. Arthur Mee wrote: 'Minehead people believe that their dance is older than the Morris and that it comes from the days when armed men used to ride little ponies to see that enemies did not land on the coast.'

There do not appear to be any accounts of the town itself being flooded in 1607. Minehead was at the time in the middle of a power struggle

Minehead Harbour.

between the Corporation and the Lords of the Manor, the influential Lutterell family of Dunster Castle.

Minehead had received its borough charter in 1559 but this was conditional upon the Corporation maintaining the harbour. In 1602, George Lutterell, describing the town's leaders as 'simple, rude handicraft men, fitter to be governed than to govern', had accused them of failing in their duties and had secured a Commission of Inquiry to investigate their actions. Behaving as if the 1559 charter had already been rescinded, Lutterell began constructing a new quay in 1604. The following year the borough's officers were arrested and brought before the Star Chamber. In 1607 the charter was declared forfeit and the town's freedoms extinguished. Attempts by the town to get a new Charter of Incorporation in 1620 and again in 1667 were defeated by the Lutterells who claimed that only they could maintain the port and that seafarers and traders were unfit for office.

The tidal wave of 20 January 1607 seems both literally and metaphorically to have passed Minehead by!

Porlock

At 1,013 feet (over 300 metres) above sea level, Selworthy Beacon is the highest point of the outlier of Exmoor that stands proudly to the west of Minehead. Beyond that, however, we come into flood-risk territory again at Porlock. The village itself is about a mile inland but the intervening ground is low and a road runs along the edge of it westwards to Porlock Weir a mile or so away.

In 1996 a storm breached Porlock's shingle ridge and dramatically changed the coastline. In a video, still to be seen on the Pathfinder Project's website, www.somersetcoastalchange.org.uk, National Trust warden Nigel Hester describes how the desolate mudflats created then became colonised by vegetation within five years. This process then accelerated and now the area is home to a wide range of flora and fauna which thrive in this new wetland habitat.

This location has always been a risk. In the eighteenth century, the road and several cottages were washed away by the sea. The danger continues; a Second World War pillbox, constructed in a 'safe' location on the edge of the beach, has now had its foundations undercut and exposed. Local fishermen have noticed in recent years that sea conditions off-shore have become more unpredictable and violent.

In an edition of BBC television's *Countryfile* programme broadcast in 2012, presenter Julia Bradbury visited Porlock, met villagers involved in the village's Flood Wardens scheme and saw preparations such as the fitting of flood barriers to cottage doors and the emergency Reception Centre at the village hall. Viewers were also given the history of the 1703 flood, though no mention was made of 1607. Ironically, this was shown on the weekend that the flooding on the Somerset Levels was at its worst and the village of Muchelney was completely cut off!

Lynton and Lynmouth

The names of Lynton and Lynmouth, about ten miles west of Porlock and over the Devon border, evoke memories of the terrible flood disaster of 15–16 August 1952. A storm described as being 'of tropical intensity' deposited nine inches of rain in twenty-four hours on the high ground of Exmoor, already saturated after a particularly wet summer. The moorland streams converging on Lynmouth were quite unable to cope with this volume of run-off. The old narrow-arched stone bridges on the West Lyn River became blocked by fallen trees, boulders and other debris and acted for a while like dams, holding back the surging waters. When they finally gave way, a wall of debris-laden water bulldozed its way through the centre of the village, where the river had previously been culverted to give more land for hotels and other businesses. Over a hundred buildings were demolished or seriously damaged, thirty-four people lost their lives and 420 were made homeless.

This was not the first time such a disaster had occurred. Similar floods had been recorded in 1796 and, significantly, in 1607.

Lynmouth (card posted in July 1951, the year before the Lynmouth Flood Disaster).

Brian Waters, in his 1955 book on the Bristol Channel, writes: 'After the eighteenth century flood wise local men avoided building new homes in the track of the old flood. The mariners of Lynmouth petitioned the Lord of the Manor to free the harbour of boulders.'

In 2001 a documentary broadcast on Radio Four suggested that the Lynmouth flood of 1952 was somehow linked to a secret government research operation, Project Cumulus, which involved cloud-seeding experiments over southern England at the time. However, there does not seem to be any hard evidence to support these allegations, but the inevitable conspiracy theories have been fuelled by rumours of government papers relating to the project being missing or destroyed.

Northam Burrows

The high rocky coastline west of Lynmouth is safe from invasion by the sea but, beyond the sand dunes of Braunton Burrows, the estuaries of the rivers Taw and Torridge offer a route inland for damaging tidal waves. At the southern end of the dangerous sand bar that has made the approach to Appledore, Bideford and Barnstaple so dangerous for shipping, Northam Burrows offers some protection from wind and wave but the dunes and flat land beyond are themselves vulnerable.

In November 2012 the *North Devon Gazette* described the urgent measures being taken to strengthen the defences. Pebbles were added to the seaward faces of the four-foot-high dunes to prevent them from collapsing. The work was necessary because during the previous month the waves had exposed part of an old refuse tip which had been in use from the early 1940s to the mid-1960s. Under the banner headline 'Time Bomb Burrows', the *Bideford Post* warned that 'a cocktail of cyanide, asbestos, transformer oil and live ammunition threatens Northam biosphere. Not only have sacks of rubbish been exposed but further along there is now a 200-yard stretch of beach where the pebble ridge has completely disappeared, leaving the waves washing along the sand dunes.'

'We are not just talking about the golf club losing a couple of greens,' said local resident Jeremy Bell. 'We are talking about the potential pollution of the whole of the estuary, the destruction of wildlife, fish, tourism and the potential overwhelming of the sea defences at Instow.'

The £3,000 scheme, the cost of which was being shared between Torridge District Council and Devon County Council, also involved moving large boulders back up the beach to the area where the rubbish

The author looking toward Northam Burrows. The water would have washed over the low land in the middle-distance.

had been uncovered. Larger lumps of rock were shipped in from further afield to complete the work. However, Mr Bell felt that this was only a temporary solution. 'Given the rate of erosion,' he wrote in the *Bideford Post*, 'the only real answer is to excavate and remove the whole tip site – which would be incredibly expensive'.

The area has an interesting history. In 1632 Torrington-born historian Tristram Risdon described it as 'lying full upon the sea, defended from the rage thereof by a ridge of chesell [shingle] where sea-holly groweth plentifully, whose roots are used as a sweetmeat and aphrodisiac'.

In his *Illustrated History of Appledore* (Volume 2, 2009), David Carter describes how:

> in Victorian times the Burrows was recognised as one of England's natural wonders and people came from far and wide to take in its bracing air. In 1850 two thousand people attended an entertainment with donkey racing, sack races and climbing the greasy pole. In 1856 five hundred people came by excursion train from Exeter 'being conveyed from the station by all possible means of transit.' In the 1880s horse races and polo matches were also held on the Burrows.

David Carter points out that 'traditionally the Burrows often flooded, as salt marshes are supposed to do. In 1896 they were reported to be completely under water as the sea rolled in a great mass of foam over the top of the pebble ridge and cattle could be seen up to their necks in water.' An embankment to protect the land here was built up by the lorry load as the refuse was tipped here from the 1940s along what became known to locals as 'The tip road'.

He describes how in 1607 'the tall North Devon cliffs hardly noticed as the extra-large wave rolled along them [but then] it entered the estuary and crashed over the pebble ridge completely covering the Burrows. Any livestock here would not have stood a chance'.

Northam Church, its tall and slender tower a prominent landmark, commands an extensive view over the Burrows and Bideford Bay. Nearby, a cairn of sixty boulders was set up to mark Queen Victoria's Diamond Jubilee. Stand here and look out across the flat land towards the Burrows and imagine the horror of anyone who happened to be on this spot on that dreadful morning 400 years ago to witness the wall of water rushing in from the sea!

Appledore
Houses in Irsha Street in the part of this little port most exposed to the incoming wave were hit head-on. Many were entirely demolished, others swamped by the water. Walls and fences were swept away as were timber and other materials from the shipbuilding yards along the waterfront. A sixty-ton vessel, fully-laden, was picked up and deposited further inland. The part of the village in the more sheltered Torridge estuary facing Instow probably fared a little better but even here there would have been considerable damage done.

David Carter's *Illustrated History of Appledore* states that 'there are no accounts concerning the aftermath in Appledore, although the Instow manor records report that a new stone quay was being built there in 1609. This can hardly be a coincidence. It probably replaced an earlier quay damaged or destroyed in 1607.'

In 1630 the Devonshire antiquarian Thomas Westcote wrote that 'this parish [Northam] is growing populous lately for, in memory of man, at a place called Appledore ... stood but two poor houses; and now for fair buildings and multiplicity of inhabitants and houses, it doth equal divers market towns and is furnished with many good and skilful mariners'.

Does this reflect the rebuilding of the place within a generation? We know it had been significant in the previous century as Leland in 1540 had described it as 'a good village' and it is plainly marked on Saxton's 1575 map. The Devon-born historical geographer W.G. Hoskins, in his masterly survey *Devon* (1954), observes that Appledore 'certainly became a populous place in Elizabethan days, rising with Bideford, having the advantage of being the first place within the bar where ships could tie up'.

Today, Appledore is a delightful place to visit but it was not always so. In the nineteenth century, West Appledore, the Irsha Street area, was notorious as the haunt of ne'er-do-wells and prostitutes. Carter writes that 'it was a lawless place. Any stranger spotted walking down the street would be lucky to escape with just verbal abuse. Locals still talk about going "over Point" to West Appledore'. My wife's three times great grandfather, William Kelly, was landlord of the Royal George pub at that time and his brother, John, had the Beaver, a rival establishment 100 yards away. When we visited the George in November 2012 we saw a photo in the bar of the pub with William standing proudly in the doorway. In 1851 two houses in Irsha Street were demolished by a heavy swell. In 1863 the waters rose two feet higher than usual, due to a strong westerly gale. Houses in West Appledore and near the Quay were flooded, according to the *North Devon Journal*, 'much to the annoyance of the inmates'. There was more flooding in 1896, when 'a fishing boat could be taken down Market Street and baulks of timber bumping through the streets had to be removed to prevent damage to houses'.

As late as 1925, Hilaire Belloc could write in *The Cruise of the Nona* of 'the startling contrast between Appledore, on the business side of the harbour, and Instow, all genteel on the farther shore. Appledore frankly a lair and Instow a desirable resort. Appledore for beer, Instow for wine. English talked in one, almost incomprehensible to the other.'

In 1607 the waterfront was close to the buildings along the quayside facing across to Instow. There were plans to widen the quay that were shelved when the First World War broke out, but with the onset of the Second World War its strategic importance was such that this was done as a priority at the cost of £27,000. In 1997 a wider promenade incorporating additional flood defences was built, slightly higher than the previous one. There are no flood marks or other relics from 1607 – the church is nineteenth century – but, as David Carter points out, the lack of pre-1607 buildings in Irsha Street is perhaps significant. The houses between the Royal George and the Lifeboat Station still look very exposed and vulnerable to storm damage. The oldest house in Appledore, one that clearly survived the disaster, is Docton Court, opposite the Richmond Dock at the other (more sheltered) end of the town, the earliest part of which is believed to date from the fourteenth century.

Instow

Breezy Instow, with its wide sandy beach, large houses and views across to Appledore, is certainly quite a contrasting place, as Belloc noted. The most interesting way to get there today is on foot or cycle along the Tarka Trail, the former trackbed of the railway from Barnstaple towards Bideford, now converted into a long-distance path. The platform and old signal box from Instow's magnificently sited station are still there, as is the jetty that was being built in 1609.

The jetty is well worth seeing. Built two years after the flood, it is a wonderfully irregular piece of stonework, photogenic from every angle. Along the promenade gaps in the wall are protected by metal barriers that can be closed to protect the road and houses beyond should a storm and new flooding be imminent.

The jetty at Instow, which was constructed in 1609. Appledore is visible across the river.

At the northern end of the village, a lane climbs up to the parish church of St John the Baptist, which stands away from modern Instow with a barton farm for company. A steep path leads up beyond the church to the graveyard. Here is another place where the visitor can stand and look out over the bay, where even on a calm day the white water of waves breaking over the bar can be picked out.

Bideford

Describing Bideford, Arthur Mee writes:

> It is hard to stand on the old bridge and watch the waters of the Torridge flowing on to the wide Atlantic or to walk on Bideford Quay without thinking of the sights that have been seen from here, for a bridge has crossed the river for at least six centuries.

There is little to see here that is actually old – certainly no memorials of the 1607 flood. However, along the quayside there are modern flood defences and across the river in East-the-Water a number of old houses in Torrington Street, alongside the river, still have barriers at their front doors to guard against flooding from the Torridge when it overflows.

The Town Quay, Bideford.

Barnstaple

David Carter writes of 1607 that 'by the time the wave reached Barnstaple much of its power had dissipated along the soft banks but the wave still brought immense chaos to the town. The waters came half-way up the houses in the main street and went right over the top of Pilton Bridge.' Pilton is now joined to Barnstaple by a road significantly named Pilton Causeway but was once a separate village whose magnificent church and attractive main street bear witness to its former independent status. There was once a wharf by the bridge, unnoticed now by the traffic on the busy road that crosses it.

Pilton Causeway was built in the middle ages to provide a dry route over the meadows north and west of Barnstaple. The name of the village comes from the word 'pill', which we have come across elsewhere, meaning a tidal creek.

For knowledge of what happened in Barnstaple itself in 1607 we are indebted to its Town Clerk, Adam Wyatt. He describes the flood as one 'the like of which was never seen in the town' and described how the water came into all the houses and cellars near the quay, burst open locked doors, demolished houses and destroyed wines and other commodities stored there.

In the Parish Registers of St Peter & St Paul's Church, the parish clerk, Robert Langdon, wrote: 'On the 20th day of January there was such a mighty storm and tempest ... that it cost much loss of goods and houses to the value of two thousand pounds, beside the death of James Frost and Sabine and Catherine, two of his children' when his house collapsed on top of them. 'The storm,' he wrote, 'began at three o'clock in the morning and continued until twelve the same day.' Interestingly, this account, with its reference to stormy weather supports the storm surge theory rather than the tsunami one. Langdon also wrote that 'in January the river at Barnstaple was so frozen that many people did walk over hand in hand from the bridge to Castle Rock with staves in their hands as safe as they could go on dry land, being the very same month the flood was.'

David Carter also quotes an account by 'another gentleman' who wrote that:

> All the houses standing upon the quay and near to the waterside are quite covered over with the flood. Barges, like water-coaches, are brought up into the streets and to men's doors, the great barques sail up and down amongst the houses. The lamentable shrieks of women, the cries of poor children, the astonishment and wild looks of all men, at the sudden alarm given by this deluge, no man can truly express.

As with Bideford, Barnstaple hides its history well and here a busy ring road makes getting into its historic centre rather difficult. Even the otherwise excellent local museum near the bridge does not seem to have anything on the 1607 flood, although modern flood-defence works show that this is still a significant issue locally, as it has always been. The Barnstaple Conservation Area Character Appraisal report (www.northdevon.gov.uk) states that a flood of 1586 'covered the marshes, tearing the roofs off houses, then sweeping them away in its path'. The twentieth-century growth of the town led to development on the flood plain of the River Yeo to the north of Barnstaple leading to flooding which has increased since the 1960s.

CORNWALL

Boscastle

The coastline of north Cornwall was too far away from the narrowing Bristol Channel to suffer in 1607. However, this does not mean that it has been immune from flooding. One of the most recent events was at Boscastle on 16 August 2004. Memorably recorded by television cameras, it was similar in its causes to the Lynmouth disaster but thankfully without the loss of life.

Like Lynmouth, Boscastle is at the seaward end of a narrow steep-sided valley which under normal circumstances is home to a small and insignificant stream, the curiously named Valency River. Just as the East and West Lyn rivers join at Lynmouth, the Valency is joined in the middle of Boscastle by another stream, the Jordan. Both rivers rise on high moorland behind the village and share a very localised catchment area. The village was known to be at risk of flooding, flash floods happening in 1827, 1950 and 1958 but, due to the sudden and localised nature of the storm, no warning was given.

A sea breeze that morning drew moist air inland where it mingled with cool dry air blowing from over the land. This resulted in a slow-moving but torrential rainstorm with over four inches (12cm) falling during the early afternoon. Just a few miles away there was no rain at all and holidaymakers were enjoying a lovely day. The ground was already saturated from earlier rains and the rivers were unable to cope. The Valency overflowed its banks at about half past three and within fifteen minutes cars were being carried away from the car park and down through the village. At its height the water level in the streets was approaching ten feet (over three metres). As at Lynmouth, the water built up behind the bridges which, blocked with debris, became temporary dams which soon gave way causing the raging waters, armed with tree trunks, branches, cars and other debris, to bulldoze their way down, damaging buildings as they went.

Yet there were no casualties. Lynmouth had been flooded at night at a time when it was impossible to summon adequate rescue services. Rescue helicopters reached Boscastle not much more than an hour after the river burst its banks and the well-trained personnel were up to the task required.

The flood level peaked at about 5 p.m. and a Visitor Centre was demolished. By six the floodwaters were beginning to recede. One-hundred-and-fifteen cars had been swept away, more than a hundred homes and businesses inundated, and four buildings demolished entirely.

Hayle

Simon Haslett and Edward Bryant, in their 2009 article about the 1607 flood, refer to one curious reference to its effects in Hayle. A handwritten note on the front cover of the 1813–1846 baptism register of St Uny's Church on the north coast reads: 'In 1607, in the reign of James the First, a dreadful hurricane happened. Perhaps a great influx of sand might have happened at Hayle.'

They are 'strongly suspicious' of the historical value of this reference 'given that this note was written over 200 years after this event.' They argue that the author might have been aware of the 1607 flood from published sources and was speculating in a very tentative manner that the sand accumulations in the Hayle Estuary might have been deposited then. 'Alternatively,' they comment, '[he] could have been recording a fading local folk memory, or transcribing from a now-lost written document.'

Mount's Bay

A tsunami whose effects were certainly felt in Cornwall was the one resulting from the Lisbon earthquake of 1 November 1755. This followed a quake, approaching magnitude nine on the Richter scale, under the seabed 120 miles south-west of the city, which was razed to the ground. About forty minutes later, a tsunami engulfed Lisbon's harbour, killing thousands of survivors of the quake who had, ironically, gathered there for safety.

Shocks were felt throughout Europe, and tsunamis later struck North Africa and even reached the West Indies. Shortly after 2 p.m. the wave, reported to be about 12ft high (3–4m), arrived in Cornwall and drowned one man (who must be considered particularly unlucky) in Mount's Bay.

There are conflicting accounts of the impact of the wave. William Borlase, the eminent geologist then living at nearby Ludgvan, recalled that 'the sea was observed to advance suddenly from the eastward'. An unnamed witness saw the sea advancing 'with great impetuosity' with 'large blocks of granite weighing six or eight tons swept along like pebbles'. A French writer, Arnold Boscowitz, referred to 'great loss of life and property on the coasts of Cornwall', but other reports fail to document any serious consequences.

In 2006, a study commissioned by Defra investigated the likely consequences of a similar event in the future. Computer modelling suggested that a wave would take about five hours to reach Britain and would have maximum wave heights of around six feet (1–2m) but rising to twice that in Mount's Bay which, like the Bristol Channel, is shaped in such a way as to focus and intensify waves.

This became more than just academic on 27 June 2011 when there were reports of a tsunami affecting the whole of the south coast from Cornwall to Hampshire. By chance this was not long after Simon Haslett had delivered

St Michael's Mount, Cornwall.

a lecture in Cornwall on the subject. The wave was quite small, no more than two or three feet in height, but fishermen in Mount's Bay observed the sea withdrawing somewhat before the wave came in – the unmistakeable warning of a tsunami. Tourists crossing the causeway to visit St Michael's Mount suddenly found themselves knee-deep in water. The change in air pressure generated static which made people's hair stand on end. There were even reports of fish leaping from the water. Higher than normal tides were reported at Newlyn and also at Plymouth and Portsmouth.

Dr Martin Davidson, a Coastal Processes expert at the University of Plymouth, said that the tsunami was probably caused by a mudslide under the sea. However, the British Geological Survey reported that there was no seismic activity in UK waters at the time.

EASTERN ENGLAND

As well as the numerous contemporary accounts relating to the Bristol Channel area, there are two contemporary sources relating to flooding in eastern England at the same time. The existence of these supports the view that a severe storm, rather than a seismic event, was the cause of the 1607 disaster.

The pamphlet *Newes From Summersetshire* goes on to state:

Just the same month of the year, week of the month and almost the same day of the week, in the county of Norfolk, not far from Kings Lynn, happened accidents, though not altogether so violent and mortal as those in Somerset, yet accompanied with much damage and no little danger.

It continues:

A couple of horse-stealers, knowing the night was a gown to cloak their villainy, came sneaking into the marsh with an intent to make a market of what was not their own and drove so many of the cattle as they thought fit up to higher grounds; but in the meantime they were hotly pursued with a fearful hue and cry – not of constables but swifter followers, viz. the waters which, having broken out at an old breach overflowed the marsh with such unrestricted violence that they were forced to leave their prey (which such fellows seldom used to do), fall to prayer and take to their heels.

All of the cattle in the marsh (being very much in number) few or none were preserved except those which they had fetched up with intent to steal; for being overtaken or rather overcome by the swiftness of the water. They were driven, some into creeks, some into bushes and some upon little hillocks and so were either lost, driven away with the water or in conclusion drowned.

The two fellows (against their wills made good), seeing what danger the water brought with it, posted to the town, raised the Sexton, got the keys of the church door and (as is the custom in such dangers) jangled the bells and with a fearful outcry raised the secure inhabitants who, imagining some house to be on fire, rose up distractedly in their shirts, crying out 'Water, Water', of which element they were no sooner up but they perceived they had too much.

Yet they were still various in their opinions, all fearing yet none knowing truly what to fear. Some got up to the steeple, many thinking thieves had got into the upper rooms of their houses, shutting their safeties out by locking themselves in. Some, thinking that it had been but a slight overflowing of a spring tide, laughed at the rest. The truth once known, it was no need to bid them to make haste, to express how amazedly men ran up and down betwixt sleep and wake, asking what news and receiving no answer but what news was stronger. In this danger, some made away with his wife, some his children, some (careless of both wife and children) hurried away his goods.

The water gave them but very short warning yet, like a merciful conqueror, having taken the town it gave them their lives, at least such as were willing to leave their goods. Some, covetous to have all, lost all for, striving to save their goods, they lost their lives.

In this night massacre some few were drowned, but their true names and certain number is not known. Up to a hill some half mile from the town they hastened where that night, or rather piece of a morning, they reposed themselves.

The next day they might behold their houses wading up to the middle in water, some calling for boats out of windows and from the steeple's top, some swimming upon planks, some on feather-beds, whom as they possibly could they relieved. Horses that were tied to mangers were all drowned, such as were swimming up and down, some recovered the land, some drowned in striving to recover it.

Although this lengthy account apparently describes a night of terror in faraway Norfolk, it is a vivid depiction of what those unfortunates in the Gwent and Somerset Levels must have gone through on the night of

30 January 1607. A description of the aftermath of the 1607 floods in Norfolk can be found on the website www.surlingham.org, describing the situation in Surlingham, a small village in the Norfolk Broads between Norwich and Great Yarmouth, and about 14 miles from the sea:

> In 1607 Surlingham suffered a lot following a flood and in 1609 an Act of Parliament was passed 'for the speedy Recovery of many thousand Acres of Marsh Grounds and other Ground in the Counties of Norfolk and Suffolk, lately surrounded by the Rage of the Sea in divers parts of the said Counties; and for the prevention of the danger of the like surrounding hereafter.' The salt water penetrated the Yare valley and affected the fishing in the river – 'whereof there was great plenty, and whereby many poor Men were maintained, and the Market served with fresh Fish are greatly decayed.' The salt would also have contaminated the grazing marshes, which were a very important part of local farming.

The areas on either side of the Severn estuary would have suffered similarly from salt contamination, making the grazing lands unusable for some considerable time.

The author of www.wherrymansweb.blogspot.co.uk, writing in 2009, speculates that the 1607 flood might be the reason for the abandonment of one of the two neighbouring medieval churches in Surlingham, but in fact P.H. Ditchfield gives the rather more prosaic answer in *Vanishing England* (1910): 'St. Saviour's Church, Surlingham, was pulled down at the beginning of the eighteenth century on the ground that one church in the village was sufficient for its spiritual wants, and its materials served to mend roads'.

Beccles in Suffolk was also affected despite being about seven miles inland from Lowestoft. The *Beccles and Bungay Times* reported that on 24 August 1940 'Dr Wood Hill entertained the Historical Society at Staithe House. Speaking of Northgate he said that in 1607 a mighty flood swept over all but its upper portion'. As at Surlingham, the flood waters must have swept up the river, inundating all the low-lying land on either side. Northgate is one of the main streets of the town, running close to the River Waveney northwards from the historic town centre to the main road where there is a bridge across the river. The street is now lined with attractive houses which appear to date from the seventeenth, eighteenth and nineteenth centuries. Are there any pre-flood survivors hiding behind later façades? Dr Wood Hill suggested that Staithe

House was 'in part probably Tudor', while 'the late Marquis of Granby, disguised by plaster, was Tudor or Jacobean'.

Further information about the 1607 flooding in East Anglia can be gleaned from www.archives.norfolk.gov.uk, which lists a facsimile document held in the Norfolk Record Office. Titled *The effects of floods in Norfolk and elsewhere in 1607*, it is described as 'a woodcut from a facsimile reprint of *A true report of certain wonderful overflowings of waters in 1607*, published in 1884. In Norfolk, the sea broke in between Wisbech and Walsoken and at Crosskeys, flooding Tilney and several other parishes within a ten-mile radius.' (Norfolk Record Office: HMN 6/323, 736X7) These are fenland parishes not far from King's Lynn, where there is no high ground to impede the flow of the flood water. Not surprisingly, flooding seems to have been frequent here, as a board in West Walton Church records floods in 1613, 1614 and 1670. The exact words are noted in Arthur Mee's *The King's England: Norfolk*:

> To the immortal praise of God Almighty that saveth his people in all adversities be it kept in perpetual memory that on the first day of November 1613 the sea broke in and overflowed all Marshland, to the grate danger of men's lives and loss of goods. On the three and twentieth day of March 1614 this country was overflowed and on the twelfth and thirteenth of September 1670 all Marshland was again overflowed by the violence of the sea.

Although the notice does not specify, it can be assumed that no one lost their life in these floods, hence the 'immortal praise of God Almighty'. An additional part of the inscription is recorded in *Suffolk and Norfolk: A Perambulation of the Two Counties* by Montague Rhodes James (1930), partly in Latin and with a rhyming translation in English:

> *Aethiopem dicas Numen laterem ve lavasse,*
> *Heu post tot fluctus sordida culpa manet.*
> Surely our Sins were tinctured in grain,
> May we not say the Labour was in vain,
> Soe many washings, still the spots remain.

Again, the contemporary view seems to have been that the floods were the result of God's wrath on a sinful nation, but that all the water had failed to wash away the sins.

The Customs House, Kings Lynn. (Joseph Pennell in *Highways and Byways in East Anglia*, 1923)

Bedford

This account from *A True Report of Certain Wonderful Overflowings of Waters in Somerset, Norfolk and Other Parts of England, A.D.1607* was edited by Ernest E. Baker for the journal *Bedford Notes and Queries*, available from 'Bedford's Virtual Library' (www.galaxy.bedfordshire.gov.uk). Significantly, it gives a different date but, at the very least, it reveals that 1607 was a rough year in eastern parts of England as well as in the west:

> The fifth of October at about midnight the water overflowed so much that men, women and children were fain to forsake their beds, and one woman was drowned. A great number of sheep, oxen, kine, horse and other cattle were lost. Amongst other there, one master cartwright gentleman, having his house enclosed round about, the water came in so much that a cart being loaded with thorns did swim about the ground. He lost by the same flood sheep and cattle to the value of a hundred pounds.
>
> The same gentleman had a gate close by the highway's side where the water ran over so extremely that at the fall thereof it made a hole forty feet deep, so that no man could pass that way without great danger. To the filling up of the said hole or pit was cast in by the men of the said town 25 loads of faggots and horse-dung filled not up the hole.
>
> Also, one Master Lee, at the Freers in Bedford, having a fair garden wherein was a great store of elm trees wherein three score were blown down. Also he had a store of coneys [rabbits] that were clean destroyed.

The Franciscans had been established in Bedford since the first half of the thirteenth century. As with leper hospitals, they were usually set up on the edge of towns where land was cheaper. The monastic church at Bedford had been consecrated in 1295 but, as everywhere else, the friary was doomed to be swept away in the Dissolution of the Monasteries and the site passed into the hands of secular owners, such as the unfortunate Master Lee. Perhaps there were still a few admirers of the old order who felt that what had happened to him was some sort of judgement that served him right!

8

WHAT IF IT HAPPENED AGAIN?

Dicmortimer's Blog, which I quoted previously, puts forward the problem succinctly:

> The uncomfortable truth for Cardiffians is that, if you were starting from scratch, you would not build a city on a flood plain at the confluence of three turbulent rivers fed by countless mountain streams in one of the wettest parts of Europe, adjacent to a funnel-shaped estuary with the second-highest tidal range on the planet.

The same could be said, in slightly more restrained tones perhaps, for Newport, Bristol, Gloucester and the densely populated lowlands on either side of the Severn Estuary. But what are the chances of the events of 1607 being repeated and what would be the consequences if it did?

In January 2007, to mark the 400th anniversary of the Great Flood, a conference was held at the Caerleon campus of the University of Newport to consider these questions. One of the participants was the risk management company RMS, whose report has already been referred to in some detail. One of the report's authors, Dr Claire Souch, Director of Model Management at RMS, warned that an 'exceptional event' on the scale of the 1607 flood – which she believes was due to a storm surge rather than a tsunami – could overwhelm the existing coastal defences:

We have run a variety of simulations of a storm surge coming up the Bristol Channel and in the worst case scenario the flood heights would be so high that they would overtop existing defences and cause flooding over an extremely large area. This could lead to damage totalling as much as £13 billion which would make it the costliest disaster ever in the United Kingdom.

She said that 80 per cent of these losses would be in Bristol, Cardiff and Gloucester but the whole of the Bristol Channel lowlands from South Wales round to North Devon would be affected.

However, Dr Souch also stated that it had to be made very clear that the chance of a repeat was small; on average such an event could be expected once in between 500 and 1,000 years. 'It's not something we can expect over the next few years – but it could happen and it last happened 400 years ago.'

She stressed that the conditions prevailing on 30 January 1607 were exceptional and were not the result of a tsunami. 'That theory has been around for a while,' she said, 'but there has been a lot of other scientific research which has now effectively disproved it'. She quoted work done by the Proudman Oceanographic Laboratory, Liverpool, which she said showed that the cause was a combination of a very high spring tide coinciding with a storm coming in from the Atlantic. This drove the waves ahead of it and pushed up a wall of water which was then funnelled up the estuary.

Others, though, remain sceptical and still believe a tsunami was responsible, in which case statistical predictions of likely recurrence become pretty meaningless. In February 2009, Paul Flynn, the MP for Newport West – an area which would be devastated by a repeat of 1607 – put down an Early Day motion at Westminster that 'this House notes the consensus expert view that a tsunami caused the flood of the Gwent and Somerset Levels in January 1607; believes that a similar event now would result in massive destruction and loss of life; and calls for an early-warning watch on the British coast'.

This provoked a caustic response from a blogger who, judging by the title of his site and the rest of its content, is a sworn enemy of Mr Flynn. His post on paulflynnisabellend.blogspot.co.uk read:

OK now, let's take a calm step back here. After all, the flood may or may not have been a tsunami in 1607, [yet] my M.P. wants to spend public money on a defence system to warn people about something that has not happened in the 400 years following the 1607 flood (and may not have happened then).

It would seem from this blog and Dicmortimer's that the nation's bloggers are violently opposed to the tsunami theory and express their opposition in tones that are less than respectful. A warning system, such as Mr Flynn proposed, is already in operation around the earthquake-prone Pacific Rim, but nothing has been done in seismically stable Britain as yet.

There should be cause for concern about the impact of another flood, whatever the source. In November 2012, after Hurricane Sandy caused massive problems in the eastern United States, Dr Tom Shaw of Ston Easton, near Bristol, expressed these worries in a letter to the *Western Daily Press*. Referring also to the East Coast floods of 1953 which ultimately led to the building of the Thames Barrier, he wrote, 'If we needed reminding of earlier events and their consequences, such as that which struck the Severn Estuary in 1607, when climate change was not the concern which it is now, New York and the media have together provided it.' He warned that the potential danger from 'the tides backed up by a marine surge which could destroy much coastal infrastructure if allowed to penetrate unhindered into estuaries like that of the River Severn' and argued for construction of a barrage which could provide vital renewable energy 'and flood protection for exposed communities such as Bridgwater, Bristol, Avonmouth, Gloucester, Cardiff and many smaller coastal communities'.

The nuclear power stations along the Severn in Somerset and Gloucestershire are a particular concern. The RMS report describes as 'salutary' what happened to the Blayais nuclear station on the Gironde estuary in France when a storm surge came up the river on 27 December 1999. 'The storm surge reached one metre higher than had been considered the maximum level possible,' it said. 'As a result the water overtopped the defences and flooded the lower level of the facility. Without any internal flood protection system, the water spread over a large network of galleries, damaging pumps and electrical circuits.'

The four reactors had to be shut down and on 5 January 2000 the French Nuclear Safety Authority admitted that there had been 'a Level 2 Emergency' at the site. It was inevitably tight-lipped about exactly what had happened but, according to RMS, 'although not confirmed, there were rumours that three out of the four cooling pumps were lost as a result of short-circuits during the surge and that the operators warned the authorities of the potential for a catastrophe'.

Blayais Power Station, Gironde, France. (Pierre-Alain Dorange, Wikipedia)

The reactors at Oldbury Power Station and at Hinkley Point, where campaigners are fighting plans for a third reactor on the site, are 'also vulnerable to being flooded by extreme water levels higher than anticipated in the design', RMS believes. Add to this the effects of flooding on the Severn Tunnel, the M4 and M5, the industrial facilities around Avonmouth, Newport and Cardiff, the effect on the nation's economy – quite apart from the impact on people's homes – does not bear thinking about.

But someone does have to think about these things, both the economic and human cost. A significant contribution to the debate comes from the PLOS (which describes itself as 'an on-line resource reporting scientific studies from all disciplines') report on 'The Effects of Flooding on Mental Health', published in 2012. The authors, Carla Stanke, Virginia Murray, Richard Amlot, Dr Jo Nurse and Professor Richard Williams reviewed the specialist literature on the subject, published in academic journals from 2004 to 2010, and concluded that 'flooding can pose substantial social and mental health problems that may continue over extended periods of time [and] can challenge the psychosocial resilience of the hardiest of people'.

Stripped of its jargon, this seems such an obvious conclusion that it hardly seems worth the effort that it took its authors to compile it but the report does address important issues such as post-traumatic stress disorder and makes recommendations for how medical and governmental agencies can reduce its effects. If another Great Flood did occur in the Bristol Channel region, its victims could be assured that expert professional counselling and other services would quickly be on hand. Whether this would improve their lot compared to the survivors of 1607, with their different level of religious belief and their everyday experience of premature death, is a moot point.

> The sea hath beaten down … a great multitude of houses, scattering and dispersing the poor substance of innumerable persons, so that the damage done – both in cattle and other goods – is supposed to amount to the value of above a hundred thousand pounds … the foresaid waters have gotten over their wonted limits, are affirmed to have run at their first entrance with a swiftness so incredible as that no greyhounds could have escaped by running before them. (*Woeful Newes from Wales*, 1607)

9

THE CONSTRUCTION
OF THE SEA WALLS

In 1829, Mr Charles Heath from Monmouth published a booklet which he described as 'the reprint of an extremely scarce and curious pamphlet of 1607'. The pamphlet was *Lamentable Newes out of Monmouthshire* and to it Mr Heath added some further information from other sources. Born in

The sea wall at Goldcliff.

Worcestershire in 1761, Heath moved to Monmouth in early life, and in 1788 set up in business as a printer in Agincourt Square. As well as being an author, printer and publisher, he was twice Mayor of Monmouth.

One of his additions to the original pamphlet was a section on the sea walls, which gives interesting details of their method of construction:

> In the hundreds of Wentloog and Caldicot have been erected upwards of forty miles in extent and, at vast expense, to keep off the sea at high tides and in stormy weather when the wind is in the south-west, otherwise the ravages would be at times very great by the inundations that would be made upon this large tract of moory land.
>
> Some of these walls are admirably built, to the height of twelve to eighteen feet and by a gradual slope falling back from the sea, faced with stone, each row of stones falling back about two inches in every foot, having a spacious embankment of earth behind the stonework. This medium of slope is found to answer best.
>
> In other parts, where the walls are not so high, some of them are made of a large embankment of earth alone, but yet more sloping on each side, so as to leave only a narrow path at the top; these being thrown up in moist weather, are covered with sods about a foot thick, and are found to be much better than those that are thinner, the grass roots having more strength. The earth of the bank not being made too smooth and close behind the sod, they soon adhere and quickly become an excellent fence to keep off the sea. The quantity of rich land lying in commons and on the marshes which these walls are built to protect is very considerable and furnish subsistence to large herds of cattle of every description.

Heath adds, 'Some idea of the extent of this inundation may be formed when the reader is acquainted that the hundreds of Wentloog and Caldicot alone are estimated at from fifteen to twenty thousand acres.'

THE COMMISSIONERS OF SEWERS

Heath also refers to the work of the Commissioners of Sewers, originally established under Henry IV, in maintaining and administering the flood defence system in this area. More details were supplied by Archdeacon Coxe in his *Tour of Monmouthshire*, published in 1801:

The justices or commissioners commonly so called are nominated by the Lord Lieutenant of the county and appointed and confirmed by the King under the Great Seal; and also by the Duchy of Lancaster under the seal of that duchy, so that in this instance, relative to the Levels in Monmouthshire, there are duplicate commissions. The term of the commission is limited to ten years, and sometimes to one more, being a year of grace. In case of emergency or public disturbance, it is conceived that the Lord Lieutenant may apply for a new commission if requisite.

The Court of Sewers at their meeting, after the issuing and receipt of the commission swear themselves into office, in pursuance of a mandate to one of them, commissioned to swear himself, by the assistance of the Clerk of Sewers, whose office is deemed very respectable. They first appoint their own Clerk who holds his office generally for life and is the Recorder of the Court. They appoint also two public expenditors; one for the level of Wentloog and the other for the two divisions of Caldicot. The office of the expenditors is to see that the walls are kept in good repair and that the reens or channels which convey the rainwaters from the hills and levels be clear of all obstructions and they are in this independent of the surveyors and jurors. To them are issued all orders from the Court relative to the taxes raised upon the levels towards maintaining the walls.

The expense is defrayed in part by lands which have been surrendered to the Court by the original possessors, because their quota towards keeping in repair the portion of the sea wall originally appointed exceeded the value of that property. The Court is obliged to accept of such surrenders, unless there be a unity of possession; that is, when the proprietors so distressed have lands elsewhere, which are not liable to a level tax. In that case the court will not accept the surrender of land so conditioned but can and does compel the proprietor, who has unity of possession, to maintain his share of the sea wall.

The two expenditors, having received in court the order relative to the sum assessed upon every acre, send their mandate to the collectors of the land tax who delivers the monies contributed by virtue of such mandate to the expenditors.

The assessment varies from two pence to six pence per acre; and the produce, after paying the expenses of the session or meeting of the court, and the salaries of the expenditors and Clerk of the Sewers, is applied to the maintenance of the sea walls. The accounts of the expenditors are annually audited by the court.

The next officers in order are the Surveyors of the Levels; of whom there is one in each parish. Their business is to present to the court defects and omissions which are overlooked or not noticed by the jurors, to repair these defects and omissions and bring in their accounts to the court. The jurors are about fifteen or more in Wentloog, three or four in every parish, and the same number, or thereabout, in each of the two divisions of Caldicot. Their office is to examine, a fortnight before the spring session, all the sea walls and reens, to make cognizance of the defects or obstructions, and to present the same by their foreman to the court in writing, which is read over by the clerk or his deputy in their presence and minutely canvassed by the commissioners. If there be any error in their presentment, they have a right to retire and amend it again to enter the court and deliver it to the Clerk, when the presentment is read and the jurors for each division and level dismissed in their turn.

In the autumn court, the accounts of the expenditors and surveyors are audited and also the accounts of particular and private expenditors, appointed by the court to supply the defects of individuals who neglect the work, and are obliged to pay those inferior expenditors a poundage of ten per cent for the money by them advanced.

In the case of any sudden accident between the spring and autumn session, a single commissioner, or more as the emergency requires, may apprise the Clerk of Sewers to cite the commissioners to examine the defects upon the spot, which is termed 'to have a view'. The commissioners immediately issue their orders for the repair as soon as possible, and even during the session. Should it appear that any difficulty arose with regard to the adjusting of the old defects, or the making of new reens or altering anything which concerns the levels at large or individuals in particular, any individual may, with the acquiescence of the court, demand a view and the case in question is finally determined by the commissioners attending.

Samuel Rudder, in his *New History of Gloucestershire* (1779), also wrote about the Commissioners of Sewers. He described how:

The lower part of the Vale from Arlingham downwards is also very liable to inundations. Commissions are occasionally held and orders and regulations made for supporting the banks of the river, on which the preservation of the country depends. In each level, to receive and carry off the water, are ten or twelve pills or inlets, which, as well as the sea wall are repaired by those whose estates lie next to them. A small sum is annually raised to defray the expense of the court of sewers by rating the parishes at 2d per acre.

He lists the acreages involved, dividing the parishes into the 'upper level' and the 'lower level': the 'upper level' includes Arlingham 738, Slimbridge 412, Hinton in Berkeley 161, Ham & Hamfallow 1,400, Hill 600, Elberton 300, Rockhampton 300, Moreton in Thornbury, 426, Oldbury upon Severn 1,247, Kington & Cowhill 300, Littleton 100 and Awre (described as 'a parish on the north-west of Severn') 200. The 'lower level' includes Aust 272, Redwick & Northwick 950, Compton Greenfield 783, Stowick 1,111, Olveston 500, Tockington 800, Over 150, Hempton & Patchway 76, Almondsbury 200, Lawrence Weston 530 and Gaunts Earthcott 116.

Rudder notes that 'in the reign of George II another commission was issued for the protection of lands lying further up the river, above these levels, but nothing was ever done in consequence of it'.

10

SOME OF THE EYEWITNESSES

We shall never know the names of most of the people caught up in the disaster of 1607. They lived and died leaving no record for posterity. However, a few names have come down to us, often because they wrote, or are mentioned in, the contemporary accounts. Their stories link them to other events of the time, helping to put the Great Flood into its historical context.

JOHN BARKER, MAYOR OF BRISTOL, 1607

The account of the flood written by Revd John Paul, the Vicar of Almondsbury, refers to villagers being rescued by boats 'sent by the Mayor of Bristol, Mr John Barker'. Clearly Mr Barker was active in assisting people then well outside the city limits.

Sadly, the traumatic events of 1607 seem to have been too much for him for he died the same year. He was buried at St Werburgh's Church in Corn Street and *Arrowsmith's Dictionary of Bristol* (1884) refers to 'an altar tomb with a figure of a civic dignitary and an inscription above, setting forth that he was Mayor and Alderman, died 1607'. John Murray's *Handbook for Travellers in Wiltshire, Dorset and Somersetshire* (1869) refers to 'a recumbent figure in his magisterial robes'. Many other mayors, sheriffs and other worthies of the City Corporation were buried at St Werburgh's over the years.

Anyone wishing to view this memorial to someone who was actively involved in the disaster relief effort following the flood is in for a difficulty. St Werburgh's was removed from Corn Street stone by stone to make way for road widening in 1878. It is not clear what the writer of *Arrowsmith's Dictionary* actually saw and where. The church was carefully re-erected in the expanding suburb of Baptist Mills, to the east of the city centre, and the district subsequently became known as St Werburgh's.

Dr Francis Godwin, Bishop of Llandaff (1601–1617)

Those who believed that the Great Flood was a judgement on the sinful would have pointed to the evidence provided by the Bishop of Llandaff (a diocese that at that time included Monmouthshire) to support their case.

Dr Francis Godwin was a scholar and historian who had been appointed bishop in 1601, following the publication of his *Catalogue of the Bishops of England since the first planting of the Christian Religion in this Island.* He had graduated from Christ Church, Oxford, in 1583, and in 1590 had accompanied the antiquarian William Camden on a tour of Wales.

In 1603, soon after the accession of King James I, Archbishop Whitgift of Canterbury wrote to all bishops asking for information on the state of their dioceses. From his detailed reply, preserved in the archives at the Bodleian Library, it is clear that Godwin had not been impressed by what he had found in his area. He stated that the clergy were widely hated and failed to set a good example to their parishioners, while sermons were only rarely preached. Perhaps this was unsurprising as the Bishop also stated that outrages were frequently committed against preachers in the form of 'verbal abuse and the laying of violent hands upon them'. Any respect owed to the clergy on account of their status had been lost because of their shortcomings. One priest, Revd Charles Lewis, Vicar of Llanllywel, was reported to have been put into the stocks at Chepstow for drunkenness. There were many unlicensed ministers officiating and unlawful marriages were common. The churches and even the cathedral were in a severe state of disrepair.

Godwin's complaints, known as his 'Injunctions', denounced 'the horrible profaning of the Sabbath everywhere by the playing of unlawful games, even at the time of Divine Service, and oftentimes in the very churchyard'. He urged people to inform on one another 'so that their offences may not escape unpunished, to the great dishonour of God'.

Bishop Godwin. (The Society of Antiquaries of London)

With the established church being in such a parlous state, it was no wonder that its rivals were doing well. Monmouthshire had the highest proportion of Roman Catholics in any diocese, apart from Chester, and nonconformity was gaining ground as well. The first organised dissenting church in Wales was to be established in Llanvaches, just outside the Caldicot Levels, in 1639.

Having read this dismal report, many Bible-believing folk would have considered the diocese ripe for blotting out in the near future! Whether Godwin said something like 'I told you so' after the flood is not recorded, but he may have been glad to quit his unpromising inheritance for the possibly more congenial diocese of Hereford in 1616. It may be significant that this appointment by the king came shortly after Godwin had published a new edition (in Latin) of his *Catalogue of the Bishops of England*, including a fawning dedication to James himself. He died in 1633.

An unlikely postscript to Godwin's career was his posthumously published book *The Man in the Moone, or a Discourse on a Voyage Thither by Domingo Gonsales*. In this book, believed to have been written sometime in the 1620s, he declared himself to be a believer in the Copernican understanding of the Solar System (in which the planets orbit the sun, the opposite of what had been the accepted belief) and adopted the principles of the laws of gravitation to suggest that mass decreases with increasing distance from the Earth.

ROBERT LANGDON, PARISH CLERK OF BARNSTAPLE (1584–1625)

Robert Langdon was parish clerk of Barnstaple from 1584 until his death in 1625. His account of the flood in which he refers to 'a mighty storm and tempest' was quoted by Haslett and Bryant in their research.

P.H. Ditchfield, in his 1907 book *The Parish Clerk*, describes how Langdon took over the post at a difficult time in the life of the church. The vicar was excommunicated in 1589 (Ditchfield does not say why) and the next incumbent fell out with the more Puritan members of his congregation. These gained support in their feud from Robert Smyth, a Preacher and Lecturer appointed and paid for by the Corporation who, it seems, respected neither the vicar nor even the Bishop of Exeter.

Smyth quickly built up a following in the parish. He picked quarrels. An extreme Puritan, he refused to wear a surplice to lead services, despite being ordered to do so by the bishop. He was inhibited (which in this

Barnstaple parish church.

context means forbidden from exercising clerical functions). In retaliation his followers made a series of wild accusations against the vicar, including being 'a companion of tipplers' and 'fooling away with his pipe and tabor'. Playing music may have provided solace for him in his troubles but his enemies obviously regarded it as a sinful distraction, and he was forced to defend himself in the ecclesiastical court.

The vicar won his case and Smyth abided by the rules for a time but some of the congregation then refused to attend services. Two of them were tried at the assizes for non-attendance and sent to jail. 'If they would rather go to jail than to church,' said the town clerk, 'much good may it do them. I am not of their mind.' The beleaguered vicar needed an ally and found one in Robert Langdon. He persuaded the Bishop to ordain Langdon as deacon, which he did in 1625, and clearly found him a tower of strength in his trials with his recalcitrant flock.

Langdon was a conscientious parish clerk and continued with these duties, which included keeping the registers of births, marriages and deaths up-to-date. He had got into the habit of adding news and points of interest to the record and it is from these notes that we have his account of the flood. He also told of a bad fire in Tiverton in 1595, a frost fair in Barnstaple in the year of the flood and another Tiverton fire in 1612. Some of his notes were written in Latin. Langdon was clearly an educated man and it is thanks to him, Town Clerk Adam Wyatt (or Wyot) and Tristram Risdon that we know so much about what happened in Barnstaple that day.

JOHN PAUL, VICAR OF ALMONDSBURY

The Reverend John Paul, vicar of the then completely rural parish of Almondsbury, to the north of Bristol, compiled a list of the parish's vicars that was later copied into a mid-seventeenth-century parish register. He also compiled annals, relating local events to national politics. His account of the Great Flood has already been quoted and provides significant detail not included in other sources:

> Unspeakable was the spoil and loss on both sides of the river. In our parish of Almondsbury four Christians perished in the water (a married man, a youth and two children). Diverse [people] went up trees and high beams in their houses and there preserved themselves until holpen with boats sent from the Mayor of Bristol, Mr John Barker, or made in the country, and with winnows … God grant that the grounds now drenched in the deep may be recovered and made fruitful again with speed, else one calamity will follow another misery as one wave of the sea doth another.

TRISTRAM RISDON

Tristram (or Tristam) Risdon was an antiquarian and topographer who was born at Winscott, which is in the parish of St Giles in the Wood near Great Torrington, in about 1580. He studied at Broadgate Hall (later Pembroke College), Oxford, but left before taking a degree due to the death of his half-sister, which resulted in his inheriting the Winscott estate. He married in 1608 and had seven children, four sons and three daughters.

From about 1605 to the 1630s he devoted his time to the study of local history and antiquities, compiling his *Survey of the County of Devon*. Unlike many other antiquarians at the time, he did not pay much attention to the family history of the nobility and his *Survey* reads more like a travel book, describing the parishes in the order in which he visited them. However, like many other contemporary authors – including the pamphleteers of 1607 – he was not above cribbing large chunks of information from earlier writers! In one of these pieces, taken from the work of Richard Hooker, he described the difficulties of using Devon's roads: 'Rough and unpleasant to strangers travelling those ways, cumbersome and uneven, among rocks and stones, painful for man and horse.'

It is not clear whether Risdon was actually an eyewitness to the flooding in Barnstaple but he certainly provides us with a vivid account:

> In the year 1607 it suffered a kind of inundation, amongst divers others on the Severn side, at a spring tide … from the ocean so high swelling that it subverted houses, drowned beasts and destroyed people, of whom some, to save their lives, were constrained from their upper rooms to take boat and be gone. The river, at some changes, and full of the moon, so overfloweth the marshes that the town seems to be a demi-island.

Arthur Mee wrote in his *The King's England: Devon* (1938):

> Buried in the churchyard [at St Giles in the Wood] is Tristram Risdon who has told us so much about Devon of 300 years ago that it is sad to find him without a memorial. For 25 years he wrote of his old county and his manuscript was copied, passing from hand to hand long after they laid him here in 1640. With its little moralisings and its quaint stories, his survey is of much interest as an ancient record.

HENRY SOMERSET (LATER THE 1ST EARL OF WORCESTER)

Woeful Newes out of Wales tells us of the selfless efforts of a privileged young aristocrat, Henry Somerset (Lord Herbert), to aid ordinary people caught up in the disaster:

> A multitude more than died, would have perished for want of food and extremity of cold, had not the Right Honourable Lord Herbert, son and heir to the Earl of Worcester, and Sir Walter Montague, Knight [of Pencoed], the brother unto the Recorder of London, who dwelt nearby, sent out boats (fetched from ten miles distant on wains) to relieve the distress. [Wains are horsedrawn carts, as in *The Hay Wain*]. The Lord Herbert going himself into such houses as he could to minister unto them provision of meat and other necessities.

It was observed that Somerset made no distinction between Protestant and Catholic victims, significant perhaps because, although brought up a Protestant, he converted to Catholicism as a young man. He was in his twenties in 1607 and went on to play a leading part in the civil war at Monmouthshire.

He was wealthy and married well. He and his wife, the Honourable Anne Russell, had nine sons and four daughters. He became a strong supporter of the Royalist cause, donating something around £900,000 from his personal fortune which had been built up by good management as much as by marriage and inheritance. In gratitude, King Charles created him 1st Marquis of Worcester in 1642. He was a popular figure in Monmouthshire, not least because he was not seen as a mere courtier but someone who looked after his tenants.

After the king's defeat at the Battle of Naseby in 1645, he asked the new Marquis to shelter him at Raglan Castle, which he did between June and September of that year. Subsequently, Raglan endured a lengthy siege by Parliamentary forces under General Fairfax. The Marquis and his Royalist soldiers endured ten weeks of constant bombardment but eventually were forced to surrender on 19 August 1646. The Marquis was an elderly man when he conducted his noble defence of the castle but when he was taken prisoner he was told that he could expect no mercy and that his property would be confiscated.

In October, Fairfax gave orders that the Marquis was to be transported to London 'in a horse-litter or some other way as he shall be able to endure the journey'. By December he was clearly soon to die. According to Jeremy Knight in *Civil War and Restoration in Monmouthshire* (2005), 'his response when told he was to be buried at Windsor is well known: "God bless us all! Why then, I shall have a better castle when I am dead than they took from me when I was alive".'

He died on 18 December and was buried in the Beaufort Chapel at Windsor Castle.

JOHN STRADLING, POET

Poet John Stradling's *Epigrams* (described as 'short poems ending in a witty turn of thought'), originally written in Latin, gave a distinctive perspective on what happened in 1607. In 1606 he wrote a poem about the sea wall at Aberthaw 'constructed for the containment of the Severn, a herculean labour completed within five months'. In 1607, he wrote another about 'the incredible flooding of the Severn, in which the sea wall, recently built at Aberthaw, was overcome and wholly torn apart'.

Sir John Stradling, born in Bristol in 1563, was adopted by a childless relative, Sir Edward Stradling, and in 1609 inherited the family estate at St Donat's in Glamorgan. He was educated under Edward Green, a canon of Bristol, and then at Oxford where he matriculated from Magdalen Hall in February 1583/4, being praised for 'the miracle of his forwardness in learning'. He studied Law for a while and then travelled abroad. His reputation for learning was such that he was admired by Camden, author of *Britannia*, and Sir John Harington, among other worthies.

He was knighted in 1608 and was created Baronet in 1611. He was MP for St Germans in Cornwall in 1623–4 and for Old Sarum in 1625. Both of these later became notorious as 'rotten boroughs' prior to the 1832 Reform Act. He was MP for Glamorgan in 1625–6. He married Elizabeth Gage of Firle in Sussex and was the father of eight sons and three daughters.

To carry out the wishes of his predecessor as MP for Glamorgan, he endowed and equipped a grammar school at Cowbridge. This endowment seems to have lapsed and the school later had to be re-founded by Sir Leoline Jenkins.

John Stradling died in 1637. His eldest son Edward (1611–1644) was one of the leading Royalists in Glamorgan at the time of the Civil War. He led a Regiment of Foot at the Battle of Edgehill in 1642. Taken prisoner, he was sent to Warwick Castle but obtained his release under an exchange of prisoners. Edward Stradling died in June 1644 in Oxford and is buried in the chapel of Jesus College.

WALTER YONGE

Walter Yonge (1579–1649) was a lawyer, merchant and diarist. His diaries cover 1604–27 and 1642–45. They are recognised as valuable historical records for these periods. They include the entry: 'The 20th January 1606–7, by reason of a great tempest, the sea broke in at divers places on the north side of this country' (by which he must have meant the northern side of the south-west peninsula). Based in Colyton in east Devon, he would not have been a witness to these events but his reference to them is testimony to how far and how quickly news of the disaster travelled.

Yonge was educated at Magdalen College, Oxford, and called to the Bar from Middle Temple. In 1628 he became High Sheriff of Devon. As a merchant he invested in the Dorchester Company, a joint-stock enterprise promoting fishing and colonisation in New England. He served in Parliament for Honiton in the Long Parliament from 1640 but was another in our story to be caught up in the turmoil of the English Civil War.

Yonge was not seen in Parliament after the notorious Pride's Purge of December 1648 when troops under the command of Sir Thomas Pride forcibly removed any Members who were not supporters of Oliver Cromwell, Thomas Fairfax and Henry Ireton, the leaders of the New Model Army. This event has been described as the only military coup d'état in English history.

11

THE MONMOUTHSHIRE MILKMAID

The contemporary pamphlets describing the flood contain a number of incidents that are not precisely located and which were too long to include in earlier chapters of this book. One such, from *God's Warning to his people of England*, concerns a milkmaid from 'a place in Monmouthshire'. It is included here, with the spelling modernised but otherwise largely unaltered, to give the flavour of the biblical style of writing that was used in these accounts:

In a place in Monmouthshire there was a maid went to milk her cows in the morning but, before she had fully finished her business, the vehemence of the waters increased and so suddenly environed her about that she could not escape thence but was forced to make shift up to the top of a high bank to save herself, which she did with much ado, where she was constrained to abide all that day and night until eight of the clock in the next morning in great distress, what with the coldness of the air and waters; and what with other accidents that there happened to her from such great perils and dangers which were likely there to ensue unto her.

But there placing herself for safeguard of her life as aforesaid, having no other refuge to fly unto, the waters in such violent sort had so pursued her that there was but a small distance of ground left uncovered with waters for her to abide upon. There she remained most pitifully lamenting the great danger of life that she was in, expecting every minute to be overwhelmed by those merciless waters. But the Almighty God, who is the Creator of all good things, when he thought meet, sent his holy angel to command the waters to cease their fury and to return into their accustomed bounds again, whereby according to His most blessed will and pleasure she was then preserved.

In the meantime, during the continuance of her abode there, divers of her friends practised all the means they could to recover her but could not, the waters being of such deepness about her and boats they had none in all those parts to succour her. Such was their want in this distress that many perished through the want thereof.

There was a gentleman of worth, dwelling near unto the place where she was, who caused a goodly gelding to be saddled and set a man upon the back of him, thinking to fetch her away, but such was the deepness of the waters that he durst not adventure the same but retired.

At last some of her friends devised a device and tied two broad troughs the one to the other (such as in those countries they use to salt bacon in) and put therein two lusty strong men who with long poles (stirring these troughs as if they had been boats) made great shift to come to her, so by this means through God's good help she was then saved.

But now, gentle reader, mark what befell at this time of the strangeness of other creatures whom the waters had violently oppressed; for the two men which took upon them to fetch away the maid from the top of the bank can truly witness the same, as well as herself, to be true, for they beheld the same with their eyes.

The Monmouthshire Milkmaid. (Catherine Cox)

The hill or bank where the maiden abode all that time was all covered over with wild beasts and vermin that came thither to seek for succour, that she had much ado to save herself from taking hurt by them and much ado she had to keep them from creeping upon her and about her. She was not so much in danger from the water on the one side as she was troubled by the vermin on the other side.

The beasts and vermin that were there were these: dogs, cats, moles, foxes, hares, coneys, yea and not so much, as mice and cats: but were there in abundance and, that which is more strange, the one of them never once offered to annoy the other although they were enemies by nature, the one to another. Yet in this danger of life they not once offered to express their natural envy but in a gentle sort they freely enjoyed the liberty of life which, in my opinion, was a most wonderful work in nature.

Perhaps the milkmaid felt that being carried off by 'two lusty strong men' was some recompense for her ordeal!

12

OTHER POSSIBLE TSUNAMIS AFFECTING THE BRITISH ISLES

Scotland, 6100 bc

The east coast of Scotland is believed to have been struck by a 70-foot high wave in about 6100 BC. This was caused by the massive underwater Storegga slides off the coast of Norway. Some of the Shetland Isles were completely submerged for a while.

The three known Storegga slides are considered to be among the largest landslips ever known. They occurred under the sea at the edge of the continental shelf. (Storegga is the Old Norse for 'great edge'.) The block that slipped is estimated to have been about the size of Iceland, involving a 290km length of shelf with a total volume of 3,500 million cubic metres. The most recent of these slips has been dated from sediments deposited by the tsunami at about 6100 BC. These deposits have been found about 80km (about 50 miles) inland along the Firth of Forth and four metres above normal tide levels.

That these massive landslips had occurred was a source of great concern when work started on exploiting the natural gas fields off the Norwegian coast. Detailed scientific investigations were carried out and it was concluded that the slides had been caused by the build-up of material deposited during the last Ice Age and that a recurrence would only be possible after another one.

ENGLAND AND WALES, 1014

The *Anglo-Saxon Chronicle* recorded a widespread flood, affecting coastal areas from Cumberland and Westmorland to Kent on 20 September 1014. It states that 'on the eve of St Michael's Day [28 September] came a great sea flood which spread wide over this land and ran so far up as it never did before, overwhelming many towns and innumerable multitudes of people'.

This flood has also been attributed to a tsunami, possibly resulting from a comet or meteorite crashing into the Atlantic. The chronicler William of Malmesbury described how 'the tidal wave grew to an astonishing size such as the memory of man cannot parallel, so as to submerge villages many miles inland and overwhelm and drown their inhabitants'. The same event is also found in some Welsh accounts.

Scientific evidence to support the theory comes from the other side of the Atlantic. Dallas Abbot of the Lamont Doherty Earth Observatory at Columbia University investigated unusual deposits, dated to the early eleventh century and found at Black Rock Forest in Cornwall, New York State. These deposits were 'difficult to explain except as an impact event'. The material seems to have originated over 3,800km away in the mid-Atlantic ridge, suggesting that it was thrown up by the impact of a comet or meteorite. Similar deposits found on some of the islands of the Caribbean supported this explanation. Furthermore, Abbot reported an 'ammonia anomaly' (an unexpected increase in levels of ammonia in the atmosphere), as observed in core samples from the Antarctic ice cap, dating from the same period. Similar anomalies are linked to known impacts of meteorites in Russia in 1908 and Brazil in 1930. It could even be 'the likely origin of the Aztec myth relating to the destruction of the fourth son by a flood, as recorded in the Aztec Calendar Stone' at the same period.

We are now entering the wilder fringes of popular science. Some enthusiasts linked a tsunami in 1014 with significant dates in the Mayan Calendar, culminating in the End of the World, predicted for (but failing to happen on) 21 December 2012. Ben Lurkin, who posted this information at www.freerepublic.com, adds that 'the date of the eve of St Michael's Day is also interesting. The Biblical accounts of Michael sound very reminiscent of an impact event: "There was war in Heaven. Michael and his angels fought against the dragon, and the dragon and his angels fought back. The great dragon was hurled down – that ancient serpent called the devil or Satan, who leads the whole world astray. He was hurled to earth and his angels with him."

'If the dragon was a comet and his angels were fragments of a comet as it broke up in the atmosphere,' suggests Lurkin, 'then the story is a perfect metaphor for an impact event. Yet this passage from the Book of Revelation was written 2,000 years ago, a thousand years before 1014. So why was 28 September already associated with Michael?' Mr Lurkin asks, before answering his own question:

> It suggests that the Earth had already experienced a previous cosmic impact on 28 September during a previous era which was the basis of the story in Revelation and the reason the date was devoted to Michael, the hero of the impact allegory. Could there be a predictable cycle of such impacts? Instead of viewing the ancient writings as prophecies, could they be closer to forecasts based on a predictable cycle?

I am not at all sure that I go along with this but it is worth quoting as evidence that, just as in 1607, people search for supernatural and mystical explanations for extreme natural phenomena such as tsunamis and devastating floods.

DOVER STRAITS, 1580

On 6 April 1580 an earthquake occurred near Calais. A study undertaken during the planning of the Channel Tunnel estimated that its magnitude was between 5.3 and 5.9 on the Richter scale. A writer at the time states:

> In the city of Calais such a horrible and terrible earthquake came to pass that a great part of the houses fell and the sea overflowed into the city and did ruin and drown a great number of houses. Numerous persons perished and a multitude of beasts were lost which were at pasture.

Ships were sunk and there were many casualties. Buildings were damaged as far away as Lille, Arras, Douai, Bethune and Rouen, as well as Ghent and Oudenarde in the Low Countries. At Beauvais the bells of the church were set clanging, to the alarm of the local populace.

Stones fell from Ely Cathedral and Westminster Abbey. Two children in London were killed by falling masonry. Puritans blamed it all on the growing prevalence of theatres in the capital which they saw as the work of the Devil. Abraham Fleming later published a collection of accounts of the quake with the somewhat forbidding title *A Bright Burning Beacon, forewarning all wise Virgins to trim their lamps against the coming of the Bridegroom; Containing a General Doctrine of Sundry Signs and Wonders, specially Earthquakes both particular and general, a Discourse of the End of this World; a Commemoration of our late earthquake on the 6 of April about six of the clock in the evening, 1580; and a Prayer for the Appeasing of God's Wrath and Indignation.* One of these accounts, by Thomas Churchyard, described 'a wonderful motion and trembling of the earth' and how 'palaces, houses and other buildings did so quiver and shake that such as were present were tossed to and fro as they stood and others, as they sat on their seats, were driven off their places'.

Worryingly, perhaps, other quakes affecting the Dover Straits occurred in 1776, 1950 and 2007.

NORTH SEA, 1858

Kent was also affected by a quake on 5 June 1858, which was also felt in parts of the Netherlands, Germany and Denmark. An eyewitness at Pegwell Bay reported classic symptoms of a tsunami: 'The sea suddenly receded about 200 yards and then returned to its former position.' Severe thunderstorms occurred on the same day in the West Country.

Researchers Jurgen Newig and Dieter Kelletat of the University of Kiel concluded that this tsunami was triggered by an underwater landslide in the Atlantic.

A NEW NORTH SEA TSUNAMI DISASTER

The scientists who carried out the research on the Storegga slides off Norway were confident that their work showed that a repeat was not going to happen. However, not everyone was so sure and an imaginative recreation of what would happen if it did was produced and can be seen on the internet (www.althistory.wikia.com). Set in 2005, it makes alarming reading:

There is a mid-sized earthquake (5.6 on the Richter scale) on the Orman Lange gas field. It is determined that drilling has destabilised the sea bed and an area two-thirds the size of Denmark and 650 metres thick slides two miles south west. The slip causes a massive tsunami which travels across the North Sea. Within an hour the entire east coast of Britain has been hit. Within two hours the wave has reached the coasts of Belgium, the Netherlands, Denmark and Germany. The Netherlands is very badly hit. The wave washes up to 75 miles inland, destroying the entire city of Amsterdam. The entire Dutch royal family and the majority of the government is killed or injured.

At its height, along the east coast of Scotland, the tsunami was 6 metres high. Inverness, Lossiemouth, Fraserburgh, Peterhead, Aberdeen, Montrose, Arbroath and Carnoustie are wrecked. The same is true of Sunderland, North Shields, South Shields, Hartlepool, Teesside and Whitby in England. The nuclear reactor at Hartlepool is surrounded by water 3 metres high. The damage causes a reactor failure and meltdown, releasing enough radioactive material to contaminate most of Teesside and North Yorkshire.

The tsunami moves south and up the Thames. The Barrier, which had been closed, is overtopped, causing major flooding in central London. The death toll in Britain is estimated at 175,000 but no-one can be sure exactly how many have died.

The authors of this alarming fantasy added the news that 'among the dead was Prime Minister Tony Blair and his wife Cherie, who were opening a new school at Seaton Carew when the tsunami struck. The PM's body was recovered three days later. Upon his death the leadership of the country passed to the Deputy Prime Minister, John Prescott, who was in his constituency, Hull. Due to the wave destroying all lines of communication, Prescott does not realise that he is in charge for twelve hours.'

The blogger who was so incensed by Newport West MP Paul Flynn's parliamentary request for an Early Warning System might take a different view after reading this account. He would perhaps be interested to know that a comprehensive system is now being put in place for the North Sea and nearby waters, although the Danish Meteorological Institute has recently reported that the risk of such an event is extremely low, no more than once in a thousand years. They thought that a North Sea tsunami would most likely be triggered by an underwater landslide in the Atlantic. The DMI suggested that while a storm can be predicted days ahead of time, with a tsunami there would only be a six hour delay before the wave hit the Danish coast.

13

PROJECT SEAL: TSUNAMIS AS WEAPONS OF WAR

Towards the end of the Second World War military scientists in New Zealand, under Professor Thomas Leech, investigated the possibilities of creating destructive tsunamis to use as weapons, presumably against Japan. Project Seal was an attempt to develop a device that could cause these, something considered to be potentially as devastating as the atomic bomb.

Over 4,000 test explosions were carried out off the Whangaparaoa Peninsula on the coast of North Island and off New Caledonia in the Pacific over a seven month period in 1945 and 1946. None succeeded in creating a wave of any significance and further research suggested that the theoretical basis of the project was unsound. The secret documents concerning Project Seal were only declassified in 1999 and were the basis of articles by Eugene Bingham, published in the *New Zealand Herald* on 25 and 28 September of that year (*See* www.nzherald.co.nz).

In 1967 the idea was taken up in *The Yo-Ho-Ho and a Bottle of Rum Affair*, an episode of Cult TV series *The Man from U.N.C.L.E.* in which agent Illya Kuryakin (played by David McCallum) led an operation to prevent the shipment of a tidal-wave machine created by deadly adversaries THRUSH as part of their dastardly scheme for world domination.

Even more bizarrely, in 2009 UFO researcher James Carron speculated that Project Seal may have been part of a clandestine American 'black-ops' campaign to fool the Soviet Union into believing that UFOs were U.S. secret weapons.

We have been carried, almost literally, into strange times and deep waters, far from the Bristol Channel of 1607.

14

A FINAL PRAYER

Reader ... I have begun and finished this business, as the short space would permit me. And now I offer it unto thee, read it with that good affection wherewith I do present it, and I am sure, it both may and will profit thee by putting thee in remembrance why God doth punish others, so that thou mayest thyself in time look unto thine own courses, lest He proceed in the same or some more grievous manner with thee; for our vices are the serpents of our souls, stinging them to death ... It is mere wickedness ... to embrace delights and past-times and neglect duty and office ... to regard nothing but idleness, riot and wanton-ness.

The Lord useth from time to time to reveal his wrath from heaven against these and other impieties. The Lord of His goodness purge our land daily more and more ... so that God's judgements being averted, we may have his mercies continually multiplied upon us and our posterity, until the world's end.

Amen.

(from *Woeful Newes from Wales*, 1607)

BIBLIOGRAPHY

Primary Sources

The easiest way of accessing the contemporary accounts are via the Great Flood website at website.lineone.net. As the preface to the site states, 'there were several pamphlets produced at the time and reprinted several times since. They are often quoted but are difficult to obtain.' This website has links to the text of three of these: *Newes out of Summerset shire*; *Lamentable Newes out of Monmouthshire* and *God's Warning to his people of England*. All these were first printed in 1607 and share some of the same text. *Lamentable Newes* is clearly copied from the Somerset one as it contains quotes from it. Both share the same woodcut illustration on the title page. *Woeful Newes from Wales* also has similar content. I found its text printed in Nichols (ed.), *Monmouthshire Medley*, vol. 2 (1977). E.E. Baker's text, *A True Report of Certain Wonderful Outpourings ...* comes from *Bedfordshire Notes and Queries* (1884). Many of these sources can also be found elsewhere on the internet.

Secondary Sources

Baker, E.E., 'A True Report of Certain Wonderful Outpourings in Somerset, Norfolk and other parts of England', (first printed at the *Weston-super-Mare Gazette*, extract published in *Bedfordshire Notes and Queries*, 1884)

Baker, T.H., *Records of Seasons, Places and Phenomena* (London, Simkin & Marshall, 1911)

Barber, Chris, *Mysterious Wales* (Newton Abbot, David & Charles, 1982)

Barratt, C.R.B., *Somersetshire: Highways, Byways and Waterways*, (London, Bliss, Sandas and Foster, 1894)

Bradbeer, John, *Exploring Barnstaple* (Thematic Trails, 2002)

Bryant, E.A., *Tsunami: the underrated hazard* (Cambridge University Press, 2001) (*see* also Haslett, S.K. and Bryant, E.A.)

Carter, David, *Illustrated History of Appledore, Vol. 2* (Appledore, self-published, 2009)

Coxe, William, *Historical Tour Through Monmouthshire* (first published in 1801, new edition Brecon, Davis & Co., 1904)

Currie, C.R.J., and N.M. Herbert (eds), *A History of the County of Gloucester, Volume 5* (Victoria County History)

Cracknell, Basil E., *Outrageous Waves: Global Warming and Coastal Change in Britain* (Chichester, Phillimore, 2005)

Davies, John, *The Making of Wales*, (Sutton, 1996, new edition The History Press, 2009)

Davies, Haydn, *The History of the Borough of Newport* (Undy, Newport, Pennyfarthing Press, 1998)

Foyle, Andrew, *Pevsner's Architectural Guides: Bristol*, (New Haven and London, Yale University Press, 2004)

Gray, Madeleine and Morgan, Prys, *The Gwent County History, Volume 3: The Making of Monmouthshire, 1536-1780* (Cardiff, University of Wales Press, 2009)

Gray, T. (ed.), *The Lost Chronicle of Barnstaple, 1586-1611* (Exeter, Devonshire Association, 1998)

Gwyndaf, Robin, *Welsh Folk Tales* (Cardiff, National Museum of Wales, 1989)

Hall, Linda J., *The Rural Houses of North Avon and South Gloucestershire 1400-1720* (City of Bristol Museum & Art Gallery, 1983)

Hall, Mike, *Monmouthshire Curiosities* (The History Press, 2010)

Haslett, S.K., 'Meteorological Tsunamis in Southern Britain: an historical review', *Geographical Review* 99 (2) pp.146-163

Haslett, S.K. and E.A. Bryant, 'Was the AD 1607 coastal flooding event in the Severn Estuary and Bristol Channel due to a tsunami?' *Archaeology in the Severn Estuary*, vol. 13 (2002) pp.163-167

——, 'The AD 1607 coastal flood in the Bristol Channel and Severn Estuary: Historical Records from Devon and Cornwall', *Archaeology in the Severn Estuary*, vol. 15 (2004) pp.81-89

Horsburgh, K. and M. Horrit, 'The Bristol Channel Floods of 1607 – reconstruction and analysis', *Weather*, vol. 61 (10) (2006) pp.272-277

Horton, Barry, *West Country Weather Book* (self-published, 1995)

Hoskins, W.G., *Devon* (Newton Abbot, David & Charles, 1954, new edition 1972)

Innes, Hammond, *East Anglia* (London, Hodder & Stoughton, 1986)

Kirby, Daniel, *The Story of Gloucester* (Sutton Publishing, 2007)

Latimer, John, *Annals of Bristol* (3 vols) (Bristol, self-published, 1900/1908, new edition

Bath, Kingsmead Reprints, 1970)

Lewis, Mark and the Young Archaeologists' Club, S.E. Wales, 'A Second Flood Mark at Redwick, Gwent, *Monmouthshire Antiquary XXIII* (2007) pp.60-66

Mee, Arthur, *The King's England: Gloucestershire* (London, Hodder & Stoughton, 1938)

_____, *The King's England: Somerset* (London, Hodder & Stoughton, 1941)

_____, *The King's England: Monmouthshire* (London, Hodder & Stoughton, 1951)

Morgan, Dennis, *Discovering Cardiff's Past*, (Llandysul, Gomer Press, 1995)

_____, *The Illustrated History of Cardiff Suburbs* (Derby, Breedon Books, 2003)

Lewis, Sian and Morris, Jackie, *Cities in the Sea* (Llandysul, Pont, 2002)

Newman, John, *The Buildings of Wales: Glamorgan* (London, Penguin, 1995)

_____, *The Buildings of Wales: Gwent/Monmouthshire* (London, Penguin, 2000)

Newport City Council, *Newport Coast Path* (publication sponsored by the Welsh Government, Cardiff, 2013)

Rahtz, Philip, *English Heritage Book of Glastonbury* (London, Batsford/English Heritage, 1993)

Rees, William, *Cardiff: A History of the City* (Cardiff City Corporation, 1969)

Rennoldson-Smith, Patricia, *The 1953 East Coast Flood Disaster: The People's Story* (The History Press, 2013)

Rippon, S., *The Severn Estuary: Landscape Evolution and Wetland Reclamation* (Leicester University Press, 1997)

Risdon, T., *The Chorographical description or survey of the County of Devon with the City and County of Exeter*, (1620, facsimile reprint of 1811 edition, Barnstaple, Porcupines, 1970)

Risk Management Solutions (RMS), '1607 Bristol Channel Floods: 400 Year Retrospective' (2007)

Roderick, A., *A Gwent Anthology* (Swansea, Christopher Davies, 1998)

Rudder, Samuel, *A New History of Gloucestershire* (Cirencester, self-published, 1779); Republished, with a new introduction by Nicholas M. Herbert; Stroud, Nonsuch Publishing, 2006)

Serle, Muriel, *Somerset: England's Green and Pleasant Land* (Melksham, Colin Venton White Horse Library, 1975)

Sheraton, John and Goodman, Ron, *Exploring Historic Dean* (Ross-on-Wye, Fineleaf Editions, 2009)

Toulson, Shirley, *Somerset* (London, Pimlico County History Guides, 1995)

Verey, David and Brooks, Alan, *The Buildings of England: Gloucestershire, vol.2: The Vale and the Forest of Dean* (New Haven and London, Yale University Press, 2002)

Waters, Brian, *The Bristol Channel* (London, Dent, 1955)

Waters, Ivor, 'Severn Ferries', in Nicholas, Reginald (ed.), *Monmouthshire Medley* (self-published, 1978)

Willis, Margaret, *The Ferry Between Newnham and Arlingham* (Alan Sutton, 1993)

Wilshire, Lewis, *Berkeley Vale and Severn Shore* (Hale, 1980)

Witts, Chris, *Disasters on the Severn* (Tempus, 2002)

Also various articles featured in the *Bideford Post, North Devon Gazette, South Wales Argus* and *Western Daily Press.*

WEBSITES

My research involved much trawling of internet sites and blogs of varying relevance and reliability. This is not a complete list but some of the most significant include:

website.lineone.net
www.rms.com
profsimonhaslett.blogspot.co.uk
www.perception9.com

www.adsb.co.uk
www.sciencedaily.com
www.burnham-on-sea.com

Most of the academic journals quoted in the bibliography are also available on-line. I also looked up internet pages on all the places and people mentioned but these sites are far too numerous to list here.

INDEX OF PLACES

If you enjoyed this book, you may also be interested in ...

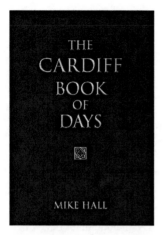

The Cardiff Book of Days

MIKE HALL

Taking you through the year day by day, The Cardiff Book of Days contains a quirky, eccentric, amusing or important event or fact from different periods of history. Featuring hundreds of snippets of information gleaned from the vaults of Cardiff's archives, it will delight residents and visitors alike.

978 0 7524 6008 6

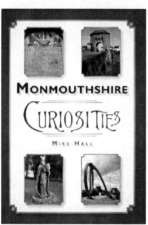

Monmouthshire Curiosities

MIKE HALL

This well-illustrated book is a guide to 100 of Monmouthshire's memorable 'curiosities'. The remarkable sights include the largest lump of coal in the world, the church which still bears the marks of the great tsunami flood of 1607, and the grave of a Rorke's Drift VC winner.

978 0 7524 4899 2

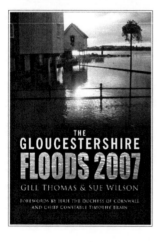

Gloucestershire Floods 2007

GILL THOMAS AND SUE WILSON

The Gloucestershire flash flooding on 20 July 2007 was catastrophic; 350,000 people were left without running water, while hundreds of homes and businesses were wrecked. This incredible book, illustrated with 100 photographs, captures the stories of local people caught up in the worst civil disaster ever to strike the county.

978 0 7509 4946 0

Visit our website and discover thousands of other History Press books.

www.thehistorypress.co.uk

Lightning Source UK Ltd.
Milton Keynes UK
UKOW04f0803120614

233278UK00001B/6/P